Motivational Interviewing for Parents

A Science-Backed Approach to Motivating Teenagers
Around Homework, Screen Time, Substance Use, and
Other Daily Battles—Without the Yelling

Jane W. Harlow

ISBN: 978-1-923646-50-6

First Edition:2026

This book provides general information and discussion about parenting and family communication. It is not intended to serve as professional psychological, therapeutic, or medical advice. The techniques and strategies presented here are educational in nature and should not replace consultation with qualified mental health professionals, particularly when dealing with serious behavioral issues, mental health concerns, or family crises.

The names and scenarios depicted in this book are purely for illustrative purposes only. Any resemblance to actual persons, living or dead, or actual events is purely coincidental. The case examples represent composite situations drawn from common parenting challenges and do not portray specific individuals.

Every family situation is unique. What works for one parent-teen relationship may not work for another. Readers are encouraged to adapt the strategies presented here to fit their own family circumstances, values, and cultural context.

If you or your teen is experiencing a mental health emergency, suicidal thoughts, substance abuse crisis, or domestic violence situation, please contact emergency services or call 988 (Suicide and Crisis Lifeline) immediately.

The author and publisher disclaim any liability arising directly or indirectly from the use of this book.

Table of Contents

Preface

When I first started researching parent-teen communication patterns, I kept hearing the same story. Loving, well-intentioned parents would describe trying everything to reach their teenagers. Rewards didn't work. Punishments didn't work. Long talks turned into arguments. Silence felt like giving up. The parents felt helpless, and the teenagers felt misunderstood.

I knew there had to be a better way.

My research led me to motivational interviewing, an evidence-based approach originally developed for counseling but with profound applications for everyday family communication. What struck me most was how this method respected both the parent's legitimate concerns and the teenager's growing need for autonomy. It wasn't about being permissive or authoritarian. It was about being collaborative.

But there was a problem. Most resources on motivational interviewing were written for therapists, full of clinical jargon and theoretical frameworks. Parents didn't need another textbook. They needed practical strategies they could use at the dinner table, in the car, or when their teenager came home past curfew.

This book bridges that gap. I've translated the research on adolescent brain development, motivational psychology, and therapeutic communication into concrete skills that real parents can use with real teenagers facing real challenges. Every technique has been field-tested. Every conversation template addresses situations parents actually encounter.

I wrote this book for the exhausted parent who's tried everything and feels like nothing works. For the parent who loves their teenager deeply but doesn't know how to talk to them anymore. For the parent who wants to prepare their child for adulthood while maintaining a relationship that will last beyond the teenage years.

The teenage years don't have to be a battleground. They can be a time of growth, connection, and transformation for both parent and child. It starts with changing how we communicate.

My hope is that this book gives you not just strategies, but confidence. Confidence that you can navigate these challenging years. Confidence that your teenager can make good decisions. Confidence that your relationship can be strong, even when things are hard.

Thank you for taking this journey. Your willingness to learn new approaches shows how much you care about your teenager. That matters more than you know.

Jane W. Harlow

Author of the best seller

Motivational Interviewing for Beginners: A Step-by-Step Guide to Creating Meaningful Change

Chapter 1.0: Why Teens Push Back

You set a reasonable rule. Your teen ignores it. You explain why the rule matters. They roll their eyes. You raise your voice. They slam their door. Sound familiar?

Here's what most parents don't realize: when your teenager pushes back against you, they're not trying to make your life miserable. They're doing exactly what their brain is wired to do at this stage of development. And the more you push, the harder they push back.

This chapter explains why traditional parenting approaches often fail with teenagers, not because you're doing something wrong, but because teen brains work differently than we've been taught. Understanding this changes everything.

1.1 Your Teen's Developing Brain

Let's start with what's actually happening inside your teenager's head.

Between ages 12 and 25, the human brain undergoes massive reconstruction. Think of it like renovating a house while people still live in it. Everything works, but not always smoothly. The teenage brain is particularly interesting because different parts develop at different rates.

The **limbic system**, which handles emotions and rewards, hits the gas pedal hard during adolescence. This part of the brain lights up like a Christmas tree when teens experience anything exciting, novel, or socially rewarding. It's why your 14-year-old will stay up until 2 a.m. texting friends but can't seem to wake up for school.

Meanwhile, the **prefrontal cortex**, which manages planning, impulse control, and considering consequences, is still under construction. This part won't fully mature until the mid-20s. So your teen has a powerful engine (emotions, desires, social drives) but the brakes (judgment, self-control) are still being installed.

Here's what this looks like in real life.

Marcus, a 15-year-old, knew he had a math test the next morning. He'd planned to study after dinner. But then his friends started a group chat about weekend plans, and before he knew it, two hours had passed. His mom found him on his phone at 10 p.m., math book unopened. "What were you thinking?" she asked. The honest answer? He wasn't thinking. His brain's reward center hijacked his good intentions. The emotional pull of social connection overpowered his ability to stick with a boring task, even though he genuinely wanted to do well on the test.

This isn't laziness or defiance. It's neuroscience.

The teenage brain is also pruning unnecessary neural connections while strengthening the ones that get used most. Your teen's brain is literally reorganizing itself to prepare for adult independence. This renovation makes teenagers more creative, more passionate, more willing to take risks, and more sensitive to peer relationships. These are actually features, not bugs. They're what help young people separate from their families and form new bonds.

But this reconstruction also means teens struggle with tasks that require sustained attention, long-term planning, and emotional regulation. They feel things intensely. Small setbacks feel catastrophic. Minor social slights feel devastating. And parental lectures feel unbearable.

Research shows that when teenagers perceive themselves as being controlled or micromanaged, their stress hormones spike (Silk et al., 2003). Their brains literally interpret parental control as a threat. This triggers the fight-or-flight response, which explains why a simple conversation about homework can escalate into a shouting match within minutes.

Understanding this doesn't mean accepting disrespectful behavior or abandoning rules. It means recognizing that your teen's pushback isn't personal. Their brain is wired to resist control right now. That's actually healthy and normal.

1.2 The Autonomy Drive

Beyond brain development, there's a powerful psychological force at work: the drive for autonomy.

Teenagers need to individuate. They need to figure out who they are separate from their parents. This isn't rebellion for the sake of rebellion. It's a necessary developmental task. Your teen must learn to make their own decisions, manage their own lives, and develop their own values. They can't do that if you're still making all the calls.

Think about it from their perspective. For their entire childhood, you told them what to wear, what to eat, when to sleep, who to play with, and how to spend their time. That made sense when they were seven. But at 15? They need to start taking the wheel.

The problem is, this transition is messy. Teens aren't ready for complete independence, but they desperately want it. Parents aren't ready to let go, but they need to. This tension creates most of the conflict in families with teenagers.

When parents try to maintain the same level of control they had when their child was younger, teens experience this as suffocating. They feel disrespected, untrusted, and infantilized. Their natural response? Push back harder.

Here's the tricky part: the more you tighten your grip, the more they resist. The more they resist, the more you worry. The more you worry, the more you try to control. It becomes a vicious cycle where everyone loses.

Consider Elena, a straight-A student who'd never given her parents any trouble. At 16, she started pushing back on her 9 p.m. curfew. Her parents couldn't understand it. "We're keeping her safe," they reasoned. "Why is she fighting us on this?" From Elena's view, the curfew made her feel like a child. All her friends could stay out until 10:30 or 11. She felt humiliated having to leave events early. More than that, she felt her parents didn't trust her judgment. The curfew became a battleground not because Elena wanted to do anything risky, but because it symbolized her parents' unwillingness to recognize her growing maturity. Every argument about curfew was really an argument about respect and trust.

Autonomy isn't just what teens want. It's what they need. Studies show that teens who have appropriate autonomy develop better decision-making skills, stronger self-esteem, and healthier relationships (Soenens & Vansteenkiste, 2010). They also have lower rates of anxiety and depression.

But here's what most parenting books get wrong: giving teens autonomy doesn't mean giving them complete freedom. It means involving them in decisions that affect them. It means explaining your reasoning instead of just imposing rules. It means listening to their perspective even when you disagree. It means letting them make choices and experience natural consequences whenever it's safe to do so.

The autonomy drive explains why "because I said so" stops working around age 12. Your teen's brain is screaming, "I need to think for myself!" When you shut down that need, you trigger resistance.

1.3 Why Punishment Backfires

Most of us parent the way we were parented. If you grew up in a household where misbehavior meant consequences, lectures, or punishment, that's probably your default approach with your own kids. And it probably worked fine when they were younger.

Then they became teenagers, and suddenly nothing works.

Lectures don't help. Grounding them doesn't change behavior. Taking away privileges creates resentment but not cooperation. What happened?

Punishment-based parenting relies on the parent having more power than the child. When kids are young, this power differential is huge. You control everything. They depend on you completely. Punishment works (sort of) because they have no choice but to comply.

But teenagers have options. They can refuse. They can sneak. They can lie. They can shut down emotionally. They can make your life miserable in countless creative ways. And they will, if they feel controlled or disrespected.

Worse, punishment damages the relationship. Every time you impose a consequence from above, you're positioning yourself as the enforcer rather than the guide. Your teen learns to hide things from you, not to come to you for help. They learn to avoid getting caught, not to make better choices.

Here's what happened with Diego and his parents. At 14, Diego got caught vaping at school. His parents grounded him for a month: no phone, no friends, no activities except school. They thought the harsh consequence would teach him never to vape again. Instead, Diego felt humiliated and angry. He didn't think about the health risks of vaping. He thought about how unfair his parents were and how much he hated them in that moment. When the grounding ended, he didn't vape at school anymore. He just got better at hiding it. He vaped at a friend's house instead. The punishment didn't address why he started vaping in the first place (peer pressure, curiosity, stress relief). It just made him more secretive and damaged his trust in his parents. When he later struggled with anxiety, he didn't tell them. He'd learned they were the enemy, not his allies.

Research on adolescent behavior change shows that punishment-based approaches often increase risky behavior rather than decrease it (Hennessy et al., 2010). Why? Because punishment creates shame and defensiveness. When people feel ashamed and defensive, they don't reflect on their choices. They justify them. They double down.

Teenagers, in particular, are exquisitely sensitive to fairness. If they perceive a consequence as unfair or disproportionate, they focus entirely on the injustice rather than on their own behavior. You want them to think, "I made a poor choice." Instead, they think, "My parents are unreasonable tyrants."

This doesn't mean teenagers shouldn't experience consequences. Natural consequences (failing a test because you didn't study, losing a friend's trust because you gossiped) are incredibly effective teachers. But imposed punishments often backfire with teens because they trigger the very resistance response we discussed earlier.

Threats work even less well. "If you don't bring your grades up, you're not getting a car." Now your teen feels controlled and resentful. They may comply out of fear, but they won't develop internal motivation. The moment your leverage disappears (they turn 18, they move out, they find their own money), the behavior you wanted disappears too.

1.4 The Righting Reflex Trap

There's another dynamic that sabotages parent-teen communication, something called the **righting reflex**.

The righting reflex is your natural urge to fix problems and correct mistakes when you see someone you love heading in the wrong direction. It comes from a good place. You care about your teen. You have life experience. You can see the consequences they can't see yet. Of course you want to jump in and fix things.

So when your teen says, "I'm thinking about quitting the soccer team," you immediately launch into all the reasons why that's a bad idea. You've paid for equipment. They made a commitment. They need physical activity. Colleges want to see consistency. What will their teammates think?

Your teen, who was maybe just thinking out loud or looking for someone to listen, now feels attacked. They dig in. Suddenly they're absolutely quitting soccer, and you're in a fight you never meant to start.

The righting reflex sounds like:

- "You should..."
- "You need to..."
- "If you would just..."
- "Let me tell you what's going to happen..."
- "The right thing to do is..."

It feels helpful. You're offering guidance, sharing wisdom, preventing mistakes. But to your teen, it feels controlling. It sends the message: "I don't trust you to figure this out. I know better than you. Your thoughts and feelings don't matter. Just do what I say."

Even when you're absolutely right about the facts, the righting reflex backfires because it triggers psychological **reactance**. Reactance is the human tendency to resist when we feel our freedom is threatened. Tell someone they can't have something, and suddenly they want it more. Tell them they must do something, and suddenly they don't want to.

This is especially strong in teenagers because of that autonomy drive we discussed. The righting reflex feels like you're trying to control them, so they resist. Even if they were already leaning toward your conclusion, your pushiness makes them want to do the opposite.

Consider Priya, a 16-year-old who mentioned to her mom that she was tired all the time. Her mom immediately went into fix-it mode: "You're staying up too late. You need to go to bed at 10. No screens after 9:30. You should eat more vegetables. Are you drinking enough water? Maybe you need vitamins." Priya, who'd simply wanted to share how she felt, now felt lectured and criticized. She shut down. "Forget it. I'm fine." She stopped sharing things with her mom because every conversation turned into a lecture. Her mom's righting reflex, though well-intentioned, closed the door to real communication.

Parents fall into the righting reflex because it temporarily relieves our anxiety. We feel like we're doing something to help. We're being responsible parents. But the long-term cost is high. Our teens stop talking to us. They stop asking for input. They make decisions without our guidance because they've learned that seeking our opinion means getting a lecture.

The righting reflex is one of the biggest obstacles to effective parent-teen communication. Later chapters will show you how to recognize it and what to do instead.

1.5 The Endless Homework Battle

Let's look at how all these factors come together in a scenario most parents know well: the homework battle.

Meet the Chen family. Their daughter Lily is 14, in ninth grade, smart enough but increasingly resistant to doing her homework. Most nights follow the same pattern.

Mom checks in around 7 p.m. "Lily, have you started your homework?"

"I will," Lily says, scrolling through her phone.

8 p.m.: "Lily, seriously, you need to get started."

"I know, Mom. Stop nagging me."

8:30 p.m.: "Lily! It's getting late. Put the phone down and do your homework now."

"Fine!" Lily stomps to her room, slams the door.

9 p.m.: Mom checks on her. Lily is at her desk but watching videos on her laptop.

"Are you kidding me right now? I thought you were doing homework!"

"I needed a break!"

"You haven't even started! Give me the laptop."

"You're so unfair! I hate you!"

This scene repeats night after night. Lily's grades are slipping. Her parents are frustrated and worried. Lily is stressed and resentful. Everyone is miserable.

Here's what's happening through the lens of everything we've learned in this chapter.

Lily's teenage brain makes homework feel nearly impossible. Her limbic system screams that social media is rewarding right now. Her underdeveloped prefrontal cortex struggles to override that immediate gratification for a delayed reward (good grades). When her mom nags, Lily's brain interprets it as a threat to her autonomy. Her stress hormones spike. Now she's not just unmotivated to do homework, she's actively resistant because doing it feels like giving in to control.

The autonomy drive makes the situation worse. Lily's 14. She desperately needs to feel like she has some control over her life. But every evening, her mom manages her homework like she's still in third grade. Check-ins every 30 minutes. Demands about when and how to work. Taking away devices. From Lily's perspective, she's being treated like a child, which makes her feel disrespected and infantilized. Her resistance isn't about homework. It's about autonomy.

Mom's punishment approach (taking the laptop, threatening consequences) backfires. Lily focuses on how unfair her mom is, not on the fact that she's failing to manage her responsibilities. She feels controlled and shamed, which makes her defensive and resentful. She's not reflecting on her poor time management. She's building resentment toward her mother.

And Mom's righting reflex is in overdrive. She sees Lily making bad choices, and her anxiety spikes. She jumps in to fix it with reminders, nagging, and ultimatums. This temporarily relieves Mom's anxiety (at least I'm doing something), but it actually makes Lily less likely to develop self-management skills. Why should Lily remember her own homework when Mom will definitely remind her? Why should Lily face the natural consequence of a bad grade when Mom will intervene first?

Three months into this pattern, the Chens are stuck. The more Mom pushes, the more Lily resists. The more Lily resists, the more Mom pushes. Lily's grades continue to drop. The relationship deteriorates. And homework, which should be Lily's responsibility, has become the family's nightly battleground.

This is where traditional parenting approaches fail. More consequences won't help. Stricter rules won't help. More lectures definitely won't help. The Chens need a completely different approach, one that works with Lily's brain development and autonomy needs instead of against them.

That's where Motivational Interviewing comes in.

1.6 What This Means

Your teenager's resistance isn't personal, and it's not a character flaw. It's a predictable result of brain development, the drive for autonomy, and how human beings respond to control.

When you understand this, you can stop taking the pushback personally. You can stop blaming yourself for "doing something wrong" and stop blaming your teen for "being difficult." Instead, you can recognize that your current approach isn't matched to how your teenager's brain actually works.

The good news? Once you understand why traditional approaches fail, you can learn approaches that actually work with teenage psychology instead of against it. You can reduce conflict, rebuild connection, and help your teen develop the skills they need for adult life.

The next chapter introduces you to an approach that was specifically designed to work with resistance, honor autonomy, and create genuine behavior change: Motivational Interviewing.

Chapter 2.0: What Is Motivational Interviewing

If you'd told me five years ago that a technique developed for treating alcoholics would transform my relationship with my teenage daughter, I would have laughed. But here we are.

My daughter wasn't drinking. She was just... unreachable. Every conversation ended in slammed doors or stony silence. I felt like I was losing her, and nothing I tried helped. Then a friend mentioned this thing called Motivational Interviewing that her therapist had taught her. "It's completely changed how I talk to my kids," she said.

I was skeptical. But also desperate.

What I learned changed everything. Not overnight. But steadily, conversation by conversation, our relationship transformed. My daughter started talking to me again. Not because I'd found some magic words, but because I'd learned to work with her psychology instead of against it.

This chapter explains what Motivational Interviewing is, where it came from, why it works, and how it's different from typical parenting approaches.

2.1 MI's Addiction Counseling Roots

Motivational Interviewing was developed in the early 1980s by two psychologists, William Miller and Stephen Rollnick, who were frustrated with how addiction counseling wasn't working.

The traditional approach went something like this: Tell people their drinking is destroying their life. Confront them with all the harm they're causing. Break down their defenses. Make them admit they have a problem. Basically, lecture them into change.

The problem? It didn't work. At all.

In fact, the more therapists pushed, the more resistant clients became. The more they confronted, the more clients defended their drinking. The harder they tried to convince someone to change, the more that person found reasons not to.

Sound familiar? It's exactly what happens when you lecture your teenager.

Miller and Rollnick noticed something interesting. The counselors who got the best results weren't the ones who pushed hardest. They were the ones who listened most. They asked questions instead of giving answers. They explored their clients' own concerns instead of imposing their own. They worked with the person's ambivalence instead of trying to demolish it.

So they developed a systematic approach built on a radical idea: people already have within them the motivation to change. The counselor's job isn't to install motivation. It's to draw it out.

They called this approach **Motivational Interviewing**, and the results were remarkable. People who received MI-based treatment were significantly more likely to reduce their drinking, stay in treatment, and maintain changes over time compared to people who received traditional confrontational counseling.

Here's what made it different. Instead of the therapist being the expert who tells you what to do, MI positions the person as the expert on their own life. The therapist's role is to help the person explore their own reasons for change, not to convince them with outside pressure.

Instead of breaking down resistance, MI works with it. When someone says, "I don't think my drinking is that bad," an MI counselor doesn't argue. They get curious. "Tell me more about that. What makes you think it's not a problem?" This curiosity paradoxically helps people examine their own thinking instead of defending it.

Instead of focusing on all the problems, MI helps people identify their own values and notice when their behavior conflicts with those values. An MI counselor might ask, "You mentioned being a good parent matters to you. How does your drinking fit with that?" Now the person is thinking about their own internal conflict, not fighting an external authority.

The approach spread far beyond addiction counseling. Researchers found MI effective for smoking cessation, medication adherence, diet and exercise, diabetes management, and countless other behavior changes. Anywhere people were resistant to change, MI helped.

And then practitioners started wondering: could this work with teenagers?

2.2 The Research Evidence

The answer turned out to be a resounding yes.

Studies show that Motivational Interviewing is highly effective with adolescents across a range of issues (Naar & Safren, 2017). Teens who receive MI-based interventions show significant improvements in substance use, risky sexual behavior, medication adherence for chronic conditions, diet and exercise, and academic engagement.

But here's what matters for parents: MI works particularly well with resistant teenagers. The very population that traditional approaches struggle with most is the population where MI shines.

Why does MI work so well with teens? Because it's specifically designed to work with the exact psychological factors we discussed in Chapter 1.0.

Remember how teenage brains are wired to resist control? MI doesn't try to control. It honors autonomy. When teens feel their choices are respected, their defensive resistance melts away.

Remember how the righting reflex backfires? MI practitioners are trained to suppress that reflex. Instead of jumping in to fix, they listen and ask questions. This creates space for teens to think through problems themselves.

Remember how punishment damages relationships? MI strengthens them. It's collaborative rather than confrontational. It positions the parent and teen on the same side, working together to solve problems.

Research specifically on parenting shows that when parents learn MI skills, several things improve (Naar-King & Suarez, 2011). Parent-teen communication becomes more open and less conflictual. Teens are more willing to discuss difficult topics. Parent stress decreases. And most importantly, teens are more likely to make positive behavior changes.

Here's what researchers found when they taught MI techniques to parents of teens struggling with various issues. In one study, parents learned to use MI approaches around substance use. Their teens showed significant reductions in alcohol and marijuana use compared to teens whose parents used traditional approaches. But the mechanism was fascinating. The teens didn't change because their parents convinced them to. They changed because the MI conversations helped them explore their own concerns about substance use and their own reasons to cut back.

Another study looked at parents of teens with diabetes who struggled with medication adherence. Parents who learned MI skills had teens with better blood sugar control. Again, not because the parents nagged more effectively, but because the teens developed their own motivation to manage their condition.

The research on MI with adolescents consistently finds effect sizes in the medium to large range, which is remarkable for any psychological intervention. More impressively, the changes tend to last. Six months, a year, even two years later, the positive effects persist.

Why? Because when change comes from within, it sticks. When you convince yourself to change, you own that decision. When someone else convinces you, you're just complying, and compliance is temporary.

2.3 How MI Differs

Let's get concrete about how Motivational Interviewing differs from typical parenting approaches.

Imagine your 15-year-old son comes home with a D on his report card in English. Here's how different approaches might handle this:

Traditional authoritative approach: "A D is unacceptable. You're grounded until you bring that grade up. No phone, no friends, nothing but school and homework. You need to understand that education matters. This is your future we're talking about. I'm disappointed in you. You're capable of better than this."

Permissive approach: "Well, English is hard. I wasn't great at it either. Don't worry too much about it. You'll do better next semester."

Motivational Interviewing approach: "A D. What's your reaction to that grade?" (pause to listen) "What do you think led to that?" (listen) "How do you feel about it?" (listen) "What matters to you about your grades?" (listen) "Where do you want to go from here?"

Notice the difference? The traditional approach imposes consequences, lectures about values, and creates shame. The permissive approach dismisses the problem. The MI approach gets curious and helps the teen think through the situation themselves.

Here's another example. Your 16-year-old daughter wants to go to a party where you know there will be drinking.

Traditional approach: "Absolutely not. There's going to be alcohol, and I don't trust you to make good decisions in that environment. You're not going, and that's final."

Permissive approach: "Well, you're almost an adult. I trust you to make good choices. Just be careful."

MI approach: "Tell me about this party. What makes you want to go?" (listen) "What concerns do you have, if any?" (listen) "I'm worried about the drinking. Can we talk about that?" (listen) "What's your plan if someone offers you alcohol or if things get out of hand?" (listen) "How can we work together on this so you get to have fun and I feel comfortable about your safety?"

The MI approach doesn't mean you have no boundaries or that teens always get their way. It means you engage them as thinking partners rather than just setting edicts from on high. You explore the situation together. You help them think through risks and consequences themselves. And you make collaborative decisions whenever possible.

Here are the key differences:

Traditional parenting operates from a one-up position. Parent knows best. Teen must comply. MI operates from a partnership position. Both people have valid perspectives and expertise.

Traditional parenting tells. MI asks. Instead of explaining why homework matters (your teen already knows), you ask questions that help them think about it themselves.

Traditional parenting focuses on problems. MI focuses on values and goals. Instead of lecturing about all the bad things that could happen, you help your teen clarify what matters to them and how their choices align or conflict with those values.

Traditional parenting tries to install motivation from the outside (consequences, rewards, lectures). MI draws out motivation from the inside (the teen's own reasons, values, and goals).

Traditional parenting sees resistance as something to overcome. MI sees resistance as a signal that you're pushing too hard, and it adjusts accordingly.

16

This doesn't mean MI is soft or permissive. You still have rules, boundaries, and expectations. But how you communicate about them changes completely.

2.4 The Four Core Principles

Motivational Interviewing rests on four foundational principles, sometimes called the "spirit of MI." These aren't just techniques. They're a way of being with another person that creates the conditions for change.

Partnership means you collaborate rather than direct. You're working together to solve a problem, not imposing your solution on your teen. This doesn't mean you have equal say in all decisions (you're still the parent), but it means you genuinely value your teen's input and involve them in the process.

In practice, partnership sounds like: "Let's figure this out together" instead of "Here's what you're going to do." It means sitting side by side (metaphorically or literally) facing the problem together instead of standing opposite each other in opposition.

Partnership acknowledges that your teen has expertise you don't have. They know how they feel, what they care about, what pressures they face, what strategies might actually work for them. You have expertise too (life experience, knowledge of consequences, resources), but neither of you has all the answers alone.

Acceptance means you meet your teen where they are without judgment. You accept their feelings, their perspective, their struggles, even when you don't agree with their choices.

This is hard for parents. Your teen says they don't care about school, and every fiber of your being wants to correct that. Acceptance doesn't mean you agree. It means you acknowledge their feeling without immediately trying to fix it or argue them out of it.

Acceptance includes affirming your teen's strengths and efforts, even small ones. It includes absolute worth (you value them as a person regardless of their choices or performance). And it includes autonomy support (recognizing their right and need to make their own decisions).

In practice, acceptance sounds like: "I can see this is really hard for you" instead of "It's not that hard, you're just not trying." It means listening to understand rather than listening to rebut.

Compassion means you actively promote your teen's welfare and prioritize their needs. Your goal is to help them, not to win arguments or prove you're right.

Compassion recognizes that behavior change is difficult and that setbacks are normal. It means you're in your teen's corner, rooting for them, even when they're struggling or making mistakes.

This doesn't mean protecting them from all consequences. Compassion sometimes means letting them experience the natural results of their choices. But it means you do so with kindness rather than "I told you so."

In practice, compassion sounds like: "I know you're trying" instead of "You're not trying hard enough." It means your tone conveys care even when you're setting a limit.

Evocation means you draw out what's already inside your teen rather than trying to install something from outside. You believe your teen has within them the wisdom, motivation, and capability to change. Your job is to help them access it.

This is the most radical shift for most parents. We're used to teaching, telling, advising. Evocation means you ask questions that help teens think for themselves. You reflect back what you hear so they can consider their own words. You help them articulate their own reasons for change.

In practice, evocation sounds like: "What matters to you about this?" instead of "Let me tell you why this matters." It means resisting the righting reflex and trusting that your teen can generate their own insights and motivation.

These four principles work together to create a relational style that reduces resistance, honors autonomy, and facilitates change from within.

2.5 From Control to Collaboration

Let me tell you about James and his dad, because their story illustrates the transformation that's possible.

James, 16, had started skipping school. Not every day, but a couple times a week he'd convince a friend to cover for him and he'd spend the day at the friend's house playing video games. His dad found out when the school called about excessive absences.

Dad's first instinct was to come down hard. Grounding, punishment, angry lectures about throwing away his future. But he'd recently learned about Motivational Interviewing in a parenting class and decided to try a different approach.

Instead of launching into the lecture brewing in his head, Dad took a breath and said, "The school called. They said you've missed a lot of days." Then he waited.

James, expecting the explosion, was caught off guard by the calm statement. "Yeah," he said warily.

"What's going on?" Dad asked. Not accusatory. Genuinely curious.

James shrugged. "School is boring. And stressful. I just needed a break sometimes."

Dad wanted to jump in with all the reasons why skipping school was a terrible idea. Instead, he reflected back: "So school feels boring and stressful, and skipping gives you relief from that."

"Yeah, exactly," James said, relaxing slightly. Someone was actually listening.

"Tell me more about the stress," Dad said.

And James opened up. The pressure to get good grades. The social dynamics. Feeling behind in some classes and not knowing how to catch up. Anxiety that felt overwhelming sometimes.

Dad listened. Really listened. He asked questions. "What happens when you skip?" "How do you feel afterward?" "What do you think about your absences?" "Where do you see this heading?"

Through this conversation, something shifted. James started thinking out loud. "I mean, I know skipping makes it worse in the long run. I fall further behind. But in the moment, I just can't deal."

"So there's a conflict," Dad reflected. "Skipping gives you short-term relief but makes the problem worse long-term."

"Yeah," James said. "That's exactly it."

They talked for over an hour. Not once did Dad lecture or threaten consequences. Instead, he helped James explore his own thinking. By the end, James himself was talking about maybe seeing the school counselor about his anxiety. Maybe getting help catching up in the classes where he'd fallen behind. Maybe developing better stress management strategies than avoidance.

Did James stop skipping school immediately? No. But over the next month, with his dad's continued support using MI approaches, he did. More importantly, he and his dad rebuilt a relationship that had been deteriorating. James started coming to his dad with problems instead of hiding them. Dad learned to listen instead of lecture. They became partners working together instead of opponents fighting each other.

This is what MI makes possible. Not perfect behavior overnight. But genuine behavior change that comes from within, paired with a stronger relationship that makes everything else easier.

2.6 Moving Forward

Motivational Interviewing offers a different way of relating to your teenager, one built on partnership, acceptance, compassion, and evocation rather than control, judgment, and fixing.

The research shows it works. Not just for reducing problem behaviors, but for strengthening relationships and helping teens develop the internal motivation and decision-making skills they need for adult life.

But understanding the principles is just the beginning. The next chapter explores the mindset shift required to actually practice MI with your teen, particularly the challenge of letting go of the expert role and trusting your teen's inner resources.

Chapter 3.0: The MI Mindset Shift

The hardest part of learning Motivational Interviewing isn't mastering the techniques. It's changing how you see your role as a parent.

For years, maybe decades, you've been the expert. You know more than your child. You teach them, guide them, protect them, correct them. This made perfect sense when they were little. A five-year-old genuinely needs you to be the expert on everything from crossing the street to brushing teeth.

But your teenager doesn't need that kind of expert anymore. They need a different kind of guide. And making that shift feels like swimming upstream, especially when you can clearly see them making mistakes.

This chapter explores the mindset shift that makes MI possible: moving from fixing to guiding, from expert to partner, from external control to supporting internal motivation.

3.1 Releasing the Expert Role

Here's a truth most parenting books won't tell you: your teenager already knows most of what you're about to lecture them about.

They know homework matters. They know grades affect their future. They know drugs are dangerous. They know screen time should be limited. They know they need sleep. They know vegetables are healthier than chips.

So why do we keep explaining these things as if they've never heard them before?

Because it makes us feel like we're doing our job as parents. Because seeing them make poor choices creates anxiety, and explaining things relieves that anxiety temporarily. Because it's what our parents did, and we don't know what else to do.

But here's what happens when you position yourself as the expert who knows better: your teen shuts down. They stop thinking for themselves because you're doing all the thinking. They stop coming to you for guidance because they expect lectures. They stop telling you things because they don't want to hear your opinion about it.

The expert role creates a one-up, one-down dynamic. You're up here with all the knowledge and wisdom. They're down there, needing to be taught. This worked fine when they were seven. At 15, it feels patronizing and insulting.

Consider what happened with Nicole and her mom. Nicole was struggling with a friend situation. Her best friend had started hanging out with a new group that made Nicole uncomfortable. She wanted to talk to her mom about it. But every time Nicole mentioned social problems, her mom jumped straight into advice mode. "Well, here's what you need to do..." "Have you tried..." "If I were you, I would..."

Nicole's mom meant well. She was trying to help by offering her wisdom and experience. But Nicole didn't need advice. She needed to think out loud with someone who would listen. After a few conversations where her mom immediately became the expert fixing the problem, Nicole stopped bringing it up. She figured it out on her own, but she lost the opportunity to process it with her mom. And her mom lost the opportunity to support her daughter during a difficult time.

Releasing the expert role doesn't mean you have no knowledge or experience to share. It means you share it differently. Instead of lecturing from on high, you offer it as information your teen can consider and decide about for themselves.

Instead of: "You need to eat breakfast. It's the most important meal of the day. Your brain can't function without proper nutrition in the morning."

Try: "I've noticed you skip breakfast a lot. I'm curious what you've noticed about how you feel on days you eat versus days you don't."

See the difference? You're not imposing your knowledge. You're inviting them to examine their own experience. They might notice they're more focused after breakfast. Or they might not. Either way, they're thinking instead of resisting.

Releasing the expert role means believing your teen can figure things out, make good decisions, and learn from mistakes. It means your job is to ask good questions and listen well, not to have all the answers.

This is terrifying for most parents. What if they make the wrong choice? What if they get hurt? What if your silence means they think you don't care?

These are valid fears. But consider this: you won't always be there to make decisions for them. In a few years, they'll be adults making all their own choices. Would you rather they practice decision-making now, while you're still around to support them through mistakes, or wait until they're on their own with no safety net?

Releasing the expert role is how you help your teen develop their own internal compass.

3.2 Trusting Inner Motivation

One of the core beliefs in MI is that people already have within them the motivation to change. Your job isn't to create motivation. It's to help them access what's already there.

This feels counterintuitive to most parents. If your teen had motivation, wouldn't they already be doing their homework, eating healthier, being more responsible? If the motivation was really in there, where is it?

It's there, but it's buried under other feelings, beliefs, and priorities. Your teen does care about succeeding in school, but that concern is currently overpowered by their exhaustion, social stress, or the immediate appeal of video games. They do care about their health, but that value is currently less compelling than fitting in with friends who vape.

The motivation is there. It's just competing with other motivations.

Traditional parenting tries to add more external pressure (consequences, lectures) to tip the scales. MI takes a different approach: it helps teens access their internal motivation by exploring their own values, concerns, and goals.

Here's how this looks in practice.

Antonio, 17, was sleeping through his morning classes regularly. His dad's first instinct was to lecture him about responsibility and create consequences. Instead, using MI approaches, he got curious.

"What's going on with the morning classes?" Dad asked.

"I'm just so tired," Antonio said. "I can't get up."

"What time are you going to bed?"

"I don't know. Midnight, maybe later."

"And what happens between dinner and midnight?"

Antonio explained: homework, video games with friends, YouTube, scrolling through social media. Before he knew it, hours had passed.

"What do you notice about how you feel when you don't get enough sleep?" Dad asked.

Antonio thought about it. "I mean, I'm exhausted. It's hard to focus. I'm in a bad mood."

"How does that affect what matters to you?"

This question opened something up. Antonio started talking about wanting to do well in school so he could get into a decent college. About wanting to be in a better mood because he'd been snapping at his girlfriend lately. About actually enjoying his morning classes when he's awake for them.

"So getting more sleep would help with things that matter to you," Dad reflected.

"Yeah," Antonio said slowly. "I guess it would."

Dad didn't lecture about sleep hygiene or tell Antonio what bedtime to have. He asked questions that helped Antonio connect his behavior (staying up late) to things he cared about (school performance, relationships, mood). The motivation to change his sleep habits was always there. The MI conversation helped Antonio access it.

Trusting inner motivation means you believe your teen cares about things, even if their current behavior doesn't reflect that. It means you help them articulate what they care about and explore how their choices align or conflict with those values.

This approach respects your teen's autonomy while also helping them develop self-awareness. They're not changing because you told them to. They're changing because they've recognized their own reasons to change.

3.3 Autonomy Fuels Development

We touched on autonomy in section 1.2, but it's worth going deeper because supporting autonomy is central to the MI mindset.

Teenagers need to practice making decisions. That's literally their developmental job right now. They need to try things, sometimes fail, reflect on what happened, and adjust course. This is how humans learn to manage their own lives.

When you make all the decisions for your teen or heavily direct all their choices, you're preventing them from developing this crucial skill. You might be preventing some mistakes in the short term, but you're creating bigger problems down the road.

Supporting autonomy doesn't mean abandoning your teen to figure everything out alone. It means involving them in decisions, explaining your reasoning when you set limits, offering choices whenever possible, and allowing natural consequences to teach when it's safe to do so.

Here's what autonomy support looks like:

Instead of: "You're taking AP History next year. It looks good for college." Try: "What are your thoughts about your schedule for next year? What are you considering? What matters to you in making that decision?"

Instead of: "Be home by 10 p.m. That's the rule." Try: "Let's talk about curfew. What time do you think is reasonable? What am I worried about? How can we find something that works for both of us?"

Instead of: "Hand over your phone. You're grounded from screens." Try: "We agreed you'd limit screen time, and I notice that hasn't happened. What's getting in the way? What do you think would help?"

Notice what's different? You're involving your teen in the decision-making process. You're treating them as a thinking person who can reason and reflect. You're not giving up your parental authority (you still have the final say on safety issues), but you're exercising that authority in a way that builds their capacity rather than keeping them dependent.

Research consistently shows that teens with autonomy-supportive parents develop better self-regulation, more internal motivation, higher self-esteem, and lower anxiety and depression (Ryan & Deci, 2000). They also make better decisions because they've practiced decision-making with support rather than having all decisions made for them.

Supporting autonomy also strengthens your relationship. Your teen feels respected and heard. They're more likely to come to you for input when they feel you treat them as a capable person rather than a child to be managed.

3.4 Understanding Teen Ambivalence

Here's something that confuses parents: your teen says they care about getting into college, but they're failing two classes. They say they want to quit vaping, but you find a vape pen in their backpack. They agree screen time is a problem, but they're still on their phone until 2 a.m.

Are they lying? Are they just saying what you want to hear? Do they not really care?

Usually, the answer is: they're **ambivalent**.

Ambivalence means having mixed feelings. Part of your teen genuinely does care about college. Another part finds homework exhausting and would rather play video games. Part of them wants to quit vaping. Another part enjoys it and feels socially connected to friends who vape. Both feelings are real. Both are true simultaneously.

This is normal and human. Adults experience ambivalence all the time. Part of you wants to eat healthily. Part of you wants the pizza. Part of you wants to exercise. Part of you wants to stay on the couch. The difference is, adults have more developed prefrontal cortexes that help us override immediate desires for long-term goals. Teens are still building that capacity.

Traditional parenting approaches try to resolve ambivalence by arguing for one side. You pile on reasons why they should care about school, hoping to overwhelm the side that wants to play video games. But here's what happens: when you argue for one side, your teen argues for the other. You push for responsibility, they defend their right to relax. You push for health, they defend their choices. This is called **sustain talk**, and it actually strengthens their resistance to change.

MI takes a different approach: it explores both sides of the ambivalence without pushing. This allows teens to examine their own mixed feelings and often resolve the ambivalence themselves.

Consider Maya, who said she wanted to try out for the volleyball team but kept missing the practice schedule. Her mom could have lectured: "You said you wanted this. Why aren't you following through? You need to commit." Instead, using MI, she got curious about the ambivalence.

"I'm noticing you haven't gone to the practices," Mom observed. "What's happening?"

"I don't know," Maya said. "I guess I'm nervous."

"Nervous about what?"

"What if I'm not good enough? What if everyone else is better?"

"So part of you wants to try out, and part of you is scared you won't measure up."

"Yeah, exactly."

Mom resisted the urge to reassure or problem-solve. Instead, she explored both sides. "What appeals to you about volleyball?" (This helps Maya articulate the change talk.) "What worries you about trying out?" (This acknowledges the sustain talk without arguing with it.)

Through this conversation, Maya got to think through her mixed feelings. She decided the want was stronger than the fear, but she needed support working through the anxiety. Mom didn't push. She created space for Maya to resolve her own ambivalence.

Understanding ambivalence means you stop seeing your teen's inconsistency as lying or manipulation. You recognize it as a normal part of the change process. And you help them explore it rather than trying to force a resolution.

3.5 Your Righting Reflex Exercise

Let's make this practical. This exercise helps you identify when your righting reflex gets triggered and what you typically do when it does.

Step 1: Think of a recent interaction with your teen that didn't go well. Pick something where you ended up frustrated, they ended up resistant, and nothing got resolved.

Step 2: Write down what they said or did that triggered your concern. Be specific. Not "they were being difficult" but "they said they didn't care about their math grade."

Step 3: Notice what you felt in that moment. Anxiety? Fear? Frustration? Helplessness? Name the feeling.

Step 4: Write down what you said or did in response. Again, be specific. Did you lecture? Threaten consequences? Try to convince them they should care?

Step 5: Consider how your teen responded to your intervention. Did they argue back? Shut down? Get defensive? Walk away?

Now here's the reflection part.

Step 6: What was your underlying fear or concern? What were you trying to prevent or fix? (Example: "I'm scared they'll fail math and it will hurt their college chances.")

Step 7: Did your response address that fear? Did it make the situation better or worse?

Step 8: What might you have said instead if you'd suppressed the righting reflex? What question could you have asked? What might you have reflected back?

Do this exercise with 3-5 recent interactions. You'll start to see patterns. Maybe your righting reflex always kicks in around school issues. Maybe it's triggered by disrespectful tone. Maybe it surfaces when you feel your teen is making unsafe choices.

Recognizing your patterns is the first step to changing them. You can't suppress a reflex you're not aware of.

Here's what this looked like for one parent:

Triggering situation: Daughter said she was thinking about quitting soccer.

Parent's feeling: Panic. Soccer has been her thing since she was six. What about the team? What about her commitment? What about her college applications?

Parent's response: "You can't quit. You made a commitment to the team. Colleges want to see you stick with activities. You're just frustrated right now, but you'll regret quitting."

Teen's response: Dug in harder. "I hate soccer. I'm definitely quitting. You can't make me play."

Underlying fear: My daughter is making an impulsive decision that will hurt her future.

Did my response help? No. It made her more committed to quitting and damaged our relationship.

What could I have said instead?: "Tell me more about that. What's making you think about quitting?" Then listen. Really listen. Help her explore her thinking rather than imposing my fears on her.

This parent later tried that alternative approach. Turned out the daughter was burned out and feeling pressure to be perfect. She didn't necessarily want to quit forever. She needed a break and some support managing the performance anxiety. By suppressing the righting reflex and getting curious instead, the parent discovered the real issue and could actually help.

3.6 The Bottom Line

The mindset shift required for MI is profound. You're moving from seeing yourself as the expert who fixes problems to seeing yourself as a partner who helps your teen access their own wisdom and motivation. You're moving from trying to control behavior to supporting autonomy. You're moving from seeing resistance as something to overcome to seeing it as information about when you're pushing too hard.

This shift doesn't happen overnight. You'll catch yourself lecturing. You'll feel the righting reflex surge and sometimes won't suppress it in time. That's normal. Like any skill, this takes practice.

But every time you pause before jumping in with advice, every time you ask a question instead of giving an answer, every time you reflect instead of direct, you're building new neural pathways. You're learning a different way of being with your teen.

And your teen will notice. Maybe not immediately. But gradually, they'll start opening up more. Resisting less. Thinking for themselves. Coming to you for support instead of hiding from lectures.

The next chapters give you specific skills and tools for putting this mindset into practice. But without the mindset shift, the techniques won't work. The spirit of MI—partnership, acceptance, compassion, evocation—is what makes everything else possible.

Chapter 4.0: Building Partnership Through OARS

The first time I tried using Motivational Interviewing with my son, I failed spectacularly. I'd learned about asking open-ended questions, so I asked him about his homework situation. He gave me a one-word answer. I reflected it back. He shrugged. I tried to affirm something. He looked at me like I'd lost my mind. "Why are you being so weird?" he asked.

I was doing the techniques, but I'd missed the point. MI isn't about following a script. It's about genuinely partnering with your teen. The skills matter, but only when they come from the right place.

This chapter introduces OARS, the foundation skills of Motivational Interviewing. Think of them as your toolkit for building real partnership with your teen.

4.1 Open Questions Create Space

Most questions parents ask are closed questions. They get yes, no, or one-word answers.

"Did you finish your homework?" "No." "Are you going to clean your room?" "Later." "Do you have plans this weekend?" "Maybe."

These questions shut down conversation before it starts. They position you as the interrogator and your teen as the suspect. Even when you have good intentions, closed questions feel controlling.

Open-ended questions can't be answered with one word. They invite your teen to think, reflect, and share. They show you're genuinely curious about their perspective, not just checking compliance.

Instead of "Did you have a good day?" try "What was today like for you?" Instead of "Are you stressed about the test?" try "What's on your mind about the test?" Instead of "Do you want to talk about it?" try "Tell me what's going on."

Notice the difference? The closed questions can be answered with yes or no. The open questions require your teen to actually think and respond substantively.

Good open-ended questions often start with: What, How, Tell me about, Help me understand, In what way.

Avoid questions that start with: Did you, Are you, Will you, Can you, Should you. These almost always lead to closed answers.

Here's what happened when Marcus learned to ask open questions. His daughter Zara, 15, had started coming home from school in a terrible mood. Marcus used to ask, "What's wrong?" She'd say, "Nothing." Conversation over.

After learning about open questions, he tried a different approach. One day when she came home scowling, he said, "You seem upset. What happened today?"

Zara paused. "Just... everything. My friends are being weird, I bombed my chemistry quiz, and Coach yelled at me for being late."

Marcus resisted the urge to problem-solve or lecture. Instead, he asked another open question: "What's the hardest part of all that?"

"Honestly? I feel like I can't do anything right. Like everyone's disappointed in me."

Now they were having a real conversation. Not because Marcus had magical words, but because his questions created space for Zara to share what was really going on.

Open questions show respect. They communicate: "I value your thoughts. Your perspective matters. I'm interested in understanding, not just getting compliance."

But here's the trap many parents fall into. They ask an open question, get a short answer, and immediately jump in with advice or another question. Your teen barely finishes speaking before you're talking again.

Real open questions require patience. Ask the question, then be quiet. Let the silence sit. Give your teen time to think. Most people, especially teenagers, need processing time. If you rush to fill every silence, you're not really opening space. You're just asking slightly different questions before launching into what you wanted to say anyway.

4.2 Affirmations Build Connection

Affirmations are not the same as praise. Praise evaluates: "Good job!" "You did great!" "I'm proud of you!" Praise comes from the expert position, judging whether something meets your standards.

Affirmations notice and appreciate. They recognize effort, strengths, and positive qualities without judgment. They come from partnership, acknowledging what you see in your teen.

Praise says: "Good job on the test!" (I'm evaluating your performance.) Affirmation says: "I notice how hard you studied for that test." (I see your effort.)

Praise says: "You're so smart!" (I'm judging your worth based on outcomes.) Affirmation says: "You have a really creative way of thinking through problems." (I recognize this quality in you.)

Why does this matter? Praise creates pressure. When you evaluate positively, teens worry about the flip side. What if next time they don't do well? Will you be disappointed? Praise makes teens dependent on your approval.

Affirmations build internal confidence. They help teens recognize their own strengths and efforts. The focus shifts from pleasing you to recognizing their own capabilities.

Good affirmations are specific and authentic. Don't just say "You're great!" Say what specifically you notice and appreciate.

"I noticed you helped your sister with her math homework without me asking. That was thoughtful."

"You've been getting yourself up on time all week. That takes discipline."

"Even though you were frustrated with that project, you kept working on it. That's persistence."

Here's Chen's story about learning to affirm instead of praise. His son Wei, 14, had always struggled with reading. Wei felt stupid, compared himself to his peers, and avoided reading whenever possible. Chen used to praise any reading: "Great job reading that chapter!" But Wei would just shrug, clearly not believing him.

Chen learned to affirm effort and specific strengths instead. When Wei finished a difficult book for English class, Chen said, "I know that book was challenging for you. The fact that you pushed through it even when it was hard shows real determination."

Wei looked up, surprised. "Yeah, it was really hard. Some parts I had to read like three times."

"That's what I mean. You didn't give up. You figured out what you needed to do to understand it, and you did it."

For the first time, Wei seemed to actually hear it. The affirmation recognized the real struggle and effort, not just the outcome. It didn't minimize the difficulty or evaluate his performance. It noticed his strength (determination, problem-solving) in action.

Over time, as Chen shifted from praise to affirmation, Wei started to see himself differently. Not as a "bad reader" who occasionally did something worthy of praise, but as someone who perseveres through challenges.

Look for opportunities to affirm:

- Effort, not just results
- Character strengths (kindness, honesty, courage, creativity)
- Progress, even small steps
- Positive intentions, even when execution was flawed
- Coping with difficult situations
- Taking responsibility

The key is authenticity. Don't make up affirmations just to say something nice. Notice what's actually there and name it.

4.3 Reflective Listening Works

If you learn only one MI skill, make it this one. Reflective listening is the secret weapon that transforms conversations.

Most of us don't actually listen. We wait for our turn to talk. While our teen is speaking, we're planning our response, formulating our advice, or preparing our rebuttal. We hear the words but miss the meaning.

Reflective listening means you take in what your teen says, process it, and reflect back the essence of what you heard. Not parroting their exact words. Not interrogating or analyzing. Simply showing you understand.

Simple reflection: Your teen says, "I hate math." You reflect, "Math is really frustrating for you."

Complex reflection: Your teen says, "Everyone's going to the party, but I don't even know if I want to." You reflect, "So part of you wants to go because your friends will be there, but another part has some hesitation about it."

Amplified reflection: Your teen says, "I'll probably just fail the test anyway." You reflect, "You're convinced there's no point in even trying."

Notice what you're not doing. You're not:

- Fixing ("Here's how to get better at math.")
- Reassuring ("I'm sure you'll do fine on the test.")
- Questioning ("Why don't you want to go to the party?")
- Advising ("You should study harder.")
- Agreeing or disagreeing ("Math isn't that bad.")

You're simply reflecting what you heard. This feels awkward at first. It seems too simple. But it's incredibly powerful.

When you reflect accurately, several things happen. Your teen feels heard, which is surprisingly rare for most teenagers. They relax slightly because they're not being judged or lectured. And crucially, hearing their thoughts reflected back helps them think more clearly about what they actually feel and want.

Here's what reflective listening looked like for Isabella and her daughter Sofia, 16. Sofia came home upset about a friend situation. In the past, Isabella would immediately jump into problem-solving mode. This time, she just listened and reflected.

Sofia: "Mia is being such a jerk. She invited everyone to her party except me and Rachel."

Isabella (old way): "Well, maybe she had limited space. Or maybe you should talk to her about it."

Isabella (reflective listening): "That feels really hurtful, being left out like that."

Sofia: "Yeah! Like, why would she do that? We've been friends for three years."

Isabella: "You're confused about why this is happening."

Sofia: "I mean, we had that argument last week, but I thought we worked it out."

Isabella: "So you're wondering if the argument is connected to not being invited."

Sofia: "Probably. She's probably still mad and this is her way of getting back at me."

Isabella: "That makes sense to you, that she's still upset about the argument."

Sofia paused, thinking. "Actually, I don't know. Maybe I should just ask her. This whole guessing game is stupid."

Notice what happened. Isabella didn't solve the problem, give advice, or even ask questions. She just reflected what she heard. Through that process, Sofia moved from upset and confused to considering a constructive action. The reflection helped her think clearly.

The key to good reflective listening is understanding the feeling beneath the words. Your teen rarely says exactly what they mean. They say, "School is stupid," but they mean, "I'm struggling and feel overwhelmed." They say, "I don't care," but they mean, "I'm scared of failing, so I'm pretecting myself."

Listen for the emotion. Listen for what's not being said. Then reflect it back gently.

Bad reflection (parroting): Teen says "I'm so tired." You say, "You're tired." Good reflection: "You're exhausted and need a break."

Bad reflection (analyzing): Teen says "I don't want to do my homework." You say, "So you're procrastinating because you're anxious about the assignment." Good reflection: "The homework feels overwhelming right now."

Practice reflective listening in low-stakes conversations first. When your teen tells you about their day, their friends, or something they watched, practice reflecting instead of responding. You'll be amazed at how conversations deepen.

4.4 Summaries Pull It Together

Summaries are like reflections on a larger scale. Instead of reflecting back one statement, you gather up several things your teen has said and pull them together, showing the big picture.

Summaries serve several purposes. They show you've been listening to the whole conversation, not just the last thing said. They help your teen see patterns in their own thinking. They provide natural transition points. And they give your teen a chance to correct you if you've misunderstood.

A good summary includes:

- Key points your teen has made
- Both sides of any ambivalence
- Any values or concerns they've mentioned
- An invitation to add or correct

Here's what a summary might sound like:

"So if I'm hearing you right, you're really stressed about your schedule. You've got soccer practice four days a week, homework is taking longer this year, and you're exhausted. Part of you loves soccer and doesn't want to let your team down. But another part is wondering if it's sustainable. You're worried about your grades slipping and never having time to relax. Is that about right? What am I missing?"

Notice the structure. You gathered multiple things Sofia said across the conversation. You included both sides (loves soccer AND exhausted). You ended with an invitation to clarify or add.

Summaries are particularly useful:

- Before making a decision together
- When a conversation is going in circles
- To mark progress in an ongoing discussion
- To transition from listening to planning
- When you need to check if you understand

Practice dialogues help cement these skills. Let's look at how OARS work together in a real conversation.

Practice Dialogue: The Grades Conversation

Dad notices his son Jamal's grades have dropped from Bs to Cs and Ds.

Dad: "Jamal, I noticed your grades this semester. What's going on?" (Open question)

Jamal: "I don't know. School is just hard this year."

Dad: "It's feeling more challenging than before." (Reflection)

Jamal: "Yeah. The teachers assign so much work. I can't keep up."

Dad: "The workload feels overwhelming." (Reflection)

Jamal: "And honestly, some of it is just boring. Like, why do I need to know about the Napoleonic Wars?"

Dad: "Some of the material doesn't seem relevant to you." (Reflection, not arguing about why history matters)

Jamal: "Exactly. So it's hard to make myself care."

Dad: "When something doesn't feel meaningful, it's harder to put in the effort." (Reflection that validates without agreeing)

Jamal: "But I know I should care. My grades matter for college."

Dad: "So there's a conflict. Part of you struggles to engage with material that feels pointless, and part of you knows grades are important for your future." (Summary showing both sides)

Jamal: "Yeah, that's exactly it."

Dad: "You've been managing to keep up with your other classes pretty well. What's different about those?" (Affirmation plus open question)

Jamal: "I like my science teacher. She makes it interesting. And math just makes sense to me."

Dad: "So when you're interested or when things click for you, you can handle the work." (Reflection highlighting his capability)

Jamal: "Right. It's just history and English I'm struggling with."

Dad: "What do you think would help with those classes?" (Open question, inviting him to problem-solve)

Notice what Dad didn't do. He didn't lecture about the importance of all subjects. He didn't impose solutions. He didn't criticize or shame. He used OARS to understand Jamal's perspective and help Jamal think through the situation himself.

4.5 Common Mistakes

Even with good intentions, parents often stumble when learning OARS. Here are the most common mistakes and how to fix them.

Mistake 1: Asking "why" questions

"Why didn't you study for the test?" "Why are you hanging out with those kids?" "Why don't you care about your grades?"

"Why" questions sound accusatory. They put people on the defensive. Your teen hears: "Justify yourself. Explain your bad behavior."

Fix: Replace "why" with "what" or "how." Instead of "Why didn't you study?" try "What got in the way of studying?" Instead of "Why are you hanging out with them?" try "What do you enjoy about hanging out with them?"

Mistake 2: Reflecting with a question mark

"You're frustrated?" "It's hard?" "You don't want to go?"

When you make your reflection a question, it sounds tentative and uncertain. It also invites your teen to just say yes or no instead of elaborating.

Fix: Make your reflections statements, not questions. "You're frustrated." "This is hard." "You're not sure you want to go."

Mistake 3: Asking multiple questions at once

"What happened? Did something go wrong? Are you upset? Do you want to talk about it?"

This overwhelms your teen. They don't know which question to answer. Usually they just shut down.

Fix: Ask one question. Then wait. Really wait. Let silence do its work.

Mistake 4: Reflecting too soon

Your teen starts to tell you something. Before they finish their thought, you jump in with a reflection. This interrupts their processing and makes them feel unheard.

Fix: Wait until they've fully expressed a thought before reflecting. If you're not sure if they're done, wait a beat longer.

Mistake 5: Affirming outcomes instead of effort

"Great job getting an A!" This evaluates results. Next time they get a B, does that mean they didn't do great?

Fix: Affirm the process, effort, or character strength. "I noticed how carefully you prepared for that test. Your planning really paid off."

Mistake 6: Using OARS as manipulation

You ask open questions and reflect, but you're just waiting to pounce with your agenda. Your teen can sense this. It feels dishonest.

Fix: Genuinely be curious. If you catch yourself using OARS to lead them to the conclusion you want, stop. Get honest about your intentions.

Mistake 7: Overdoing it

Every sentence becomes a reflection. "You seem tired." "You said you're tired." "So you're experiencing tiredness." It becomes robotic and weird.

Fix: Be natural. Mix reflections with normal conversation. Use OARS intentionally, not constantly.

4.6 Putting It Together

OARS skills work best when combined fluidly. You're not following a rigid formula. You're building genuine partnership through curiosity (open questions), recognition (affirmations), understanding (reflections), and synthesis (summaries).

Practice with low-stakes conversations first. When your teen tells you about a movie they watched or a game they played, practice OARS. Ask open questions about what they enjoyed. Reflect their enthusiasm or frustration. Affirm their insights or knowledge about the topic. Summarize what they've shared.

This builds muscle memory. When harder conversations come up, the skills will feel more natural.

The goal isn't perfection. You'll ask closed questions sometimes. You'll jump in with advice. You'll forget to reflect. That's normal. What matters is the overall direction. Are you moving toward genuine curiosity and partnership? Are you letting your teen's perspective matter? Are you creating space for them to think?

OARS gives you tools to do that. But remember, the tools only work when they come from the MI spirit we discussed in section 2.4. Partnership, acceptance, compassion, evocation. The techniques serve that spirit, not the other way around.

4.7 Next Steps

You now have the foundational skills. The next chapter builds on OARS to teach you something more nuanced: how to help your teen talk themselves into positive changes by recognizing and eliciting change talk.

But before moving on, practice OARS this week. Pick one skill to focus on each day. Monday, practice open questions. Tuesday, practice affirmations. Wednesday through Friday, practice reflective listening. Notice what happens when you consistently use these skills.

Chapter 5.0: Creating Change Talk

"I know I should study more, but..." "I really need to get more sleep, but..." "I want to get better grades, but..."

Your teen says these things, and you hear the "but" as an excuse. So you jump in to argue with it. You explain why the "but" doesn't matter, why they really should study or sleep or whatever it is.

And they dig in harder on the "but."

Here's what you missed: the first part of that sentence was gold. "I know I should study more" is change talk. Your teen just told you they recognize a need to change. But instead of building on that, you argued with the resistance part, which only strengthened it.

This chapter teaches you to recognize change talk when it appears and, more importantly, how to draw it out strategically.

5.1 Recognizing Change Talk

Change talk is any statement your teen makes that favors movement toward a positive change. It's them arguing for change, not you arguing for it.

The power of change talk lies in a simple psychological principle: we believe what we hear ourselves say. When your teen articulates their own reasons for change, their own desires to be different, their own abilities to make it happen, they're convincing themselves.

Change talk sounds like:

- "I should probably..."
- "I want to..."
- "I need to..."
- "It would be better if I..."
- "I could..."
- "I'm thinking about..."

The opposite is **sustain talk**, statements that favor staying the same or defending the problem behavior.

Sustain talk sounds like:

- "I can't..."
- "It's too hard..."
- "I don't need to..."
- "It's not a big deal..."
- "Everyone else does it..."

Both change talk and sustain talk are normal. Remember in section 3.4, we discussed ambivalence. Your teen has mixed feelings. Part of them wants to change, part of them wants to stay the same. They'll express both in the same conversation, sometimes in the same sentence.

The key is what you do with each type of talk. When you hear change talk, you want to strengthen it. When you hear sustain talk, you want to soften it without arguing against it.

Here's what this looked like for Nicole and her son David, 15. David mentioned he was thinking about trying out for the track team. This is change talk (thinking about a new positive behavior). Nicole got excited and started pushing: "That's great! You should definitely do it! It would be so good for you!"

David immediately backed off. "I don't know. I'm probably not fast enough anyway."

Nicole's enthusiasm actually triggered sustain talk. By pushing too hard on the change talk, she created resistance.

If she'd understood change talk dynamics, she might have responded differently: "You're considering track. What appeals to you about it?" This invites David to articulate more change talk (his own reasons for considering it) instead of defending against her enthusiasm.

5.2 The DARN CAT Framework

There's a useful acronym for recognizing different types of change talk: DARN CAT. This gives you categories to listen for.

D - Desire: Statements about wanting change. "I wish I could get better grades." "I'd like to have more energy." "I want my parents to trust me more."

A - Ability: Statements about capability. "I could study more if I wanted to." "I'm able to wake up earlier." "I know how to manage my time better."

R - Reasons: Statements about why change matters. "My grades affect my college options." "I feel better when I exercise." "Lying to my parents makes me feel guilty."

N - Need: Statements about necessity or importance. "I need to get more organized." "I have to start taking this seriously." "It's important that I fix this."

Those four (DARN) are **preparatory change talk**. They show your teen is thinking about change, getting ready, but not yet committed.

The second part of the acronym (CAT) represents **mobilizing change talk**, which shows stronger commitment.

C - Commitment: Statements of intention or decision. "I'm going to start studying right after dinner." "I will talk to my teacher about extra credit." "I promise I'll be home by curfew."

A - Activation: Statements showing readiness. "I'm ready to make a change." "I'm prepared to do what it takes." "I'm willing to try a different approach."

T - Taking Steps: Statements about actions already taken. "I already deleted the app from my phone." "I talked to my counselor about it today." "I've started going to bed earlier this week."

As you listen to your teen, notice what type of change talk they're expressing. Early in a conversation, you'll mostly hear DARN (preparatory change talk). As they get clearer about wanting to change, you'll start hearing CAT (mobilizing change talk).

Your job is to recognize change talk and strengthen it, while gently softening sustain talk.

5.3 Eliciting Change Talk

You can strategically ask questions that make change talk more likely. These questions don't manipulate or trick your teen. They simply invite them to consider perspectives that might generate their own motivation.

Evocative questions invite change talk:

"What concerns you about [current situation]?" "What would be the benefits of [positive change]?" "How would things be better if you [changed behavior]?" "What makes you think you might need to [make a change]?" "If you decided to [change], what would be your reasons?"

Notice these questions assume nothing. They don't presume your teen wants to change or agrees there's a problem. They simply invite exploration.

Here's how Aisha used evocative questions with her daughter Layla, 14, about excessive screen time. Instead of lecturing about phone addiction, Aisha got curious.

Aisha: "What do you notice about how you feel when you've been on your phone for a long time?"

Layla: "I don't know. Fine, I guess."

Aisha: "So it doesn't affect how you feel at all?" (Reflection with amplification, gently testing)

Layla: "Well, sometimes my eyes hurt. And I feel kind of... blah after scrolling for hours."

Aisha: "Your eyes hurt and you feel kind of flat." (Reflection)

Layla: "Yeah. And then I realize I wasted like three hours."

Aisha: "So part of you feels like that time wasn't well spent." (Reflection identifying change talk)

Layla: "I mean, I could have been doing other stuff. But it's just easy to get sucked in."

Aisha: "What kinds of other stuff do you wish you had time for?" (Open question inviting more change talk)

Layla: "I used to draw all the time. I haven't drawn anything in like two months."

Aisha: "Drawing used to be important to you." (Reflection)

Layla: "Yeah. I really miss it actually."

Aisha: "If you had more time for drawing, how would that feel?" (Evocative question)

Layla: "Good. Like I was actually doing something instead of just... consuming stuff."

Notice what Aisha did. She didn't lecture. She didn't argue that phone use was bad. She asked questions that helped Layla articulate her own concerns (eyes hurt, time wasted, missing drawing) and her own values (wanting to create rather than just consume). Layla talked herself into recognizing that her screen time was costing her something she valued.

Other powerful evocative questions:

"Looking ahead to next year, what would you like to be different?" "If you could change one thing about the current situation, what would it be?" "What are your best hopes for how this might work out?" "On a scale of 1 to 10, how important is [change] to you? What makes it a [number they said] and not a 0?" "What's the next step, if you were to decide to make a change?"

These questions all do the same thing: they invite your teen to generate their own change talk.

5.4 Responding to Change Talk

When you hear change talk, your job is to strengthen it. You do this through OARS, particularly reflections.

When your teen says something that favors change, reflect it back. This makes them hear it again, which reinforces it.

Teen: "I guess I should probably start studying earlier instead of cramming the night before."

Parent reflection: "You're thinking earlier study sessions would work better than last-minute cramming."

Teen: "Yeah, I always feel so stressed when I wait until the last minute."

Parent reflection: "So there's a real cost to procrastinating, the stress isn't worth it."

Teen: "Exactly. And I don't actually learn the material as well."

Notice what's happening. Each reflection invites the teen to elaborate on their change talk. They're building their own case for change, convincing themselves.

You can also use open questions to strengthen change talk:

Teen: "I think I need to get more organized."

Parent: "What would being more organized do for you?" (Invites them to articulate benefits)

Teen: "I'd feel less scattered. I wouldn't forget assignments."

Parent: "Feeling more on top of things matters to you." (Reflection affirming their value)

Another powerful response to change talk is asking for elaboration:

Teen: "I want to do better in school."

Parent: "Tell me more about that. What would 'doing better' look like for you?"

This invites them to get specific about their change talk, making it more real and concrete.

You can also ask about past success:

Teen: "I don't think I can wake up earlier."

Parent: "Was there ever a time when you did manage to wake up early consistently? What was different then?"

This helps them identify their own capabilities and resources.

5.5 Handling Sustain Talk

When you hear sustain talk (defending the problem or resisting change), your instinct is to argue against it. Resist that instinct.

If you argue with sustain talk, you strengthen it. Remember the psychological reactance we discussed in section 1.4. When you argue for one side, your teen argues for the other.

Teen: "Screen time isn't even a real problem. Everyone I know is on their phone as much as me."

Parent (arguing): "That doesn't make it okay! Just because everyone else wastes time doesn't mean you should!"

Teen: "I'm not wasting time. I'm staying connected with my friends."

Parent: "You could connect in person instead of through a screen!"

Teen: "You just don't understand how people communicate now."

See how the arguing escalated? The more the parent argued against screen time, the more the teen defended it. This is exactly what you don't want.

Instead, use reflection to soften sustain talk without arguing against it.

Teen: "Screen time isn't even a real problem. Everyone I know is on their phone as much as me."

Parent (reflecting): "It doesn't feel like a problem to you since it's normal for your peer group."

Teen: "Exactly. It's just what we do."

Parent: "And at the same time, you mentioned earlier that you miss drawing." (Reflection pivoting to earlier change talk)

Teen: (pauses) "Yeah, I do miss that."

Parent: "So maybe it's not as simple as whether it's a problem or not. Maybe it's more about whether you're spending your time the way you really want to." (Reframing)

Notice the difference. The parent didn't argue against the sustain talk. She reflected it neutrally, then pivoted back to change talk (missing drawing) and reframed the issue in a way that invites reflection.

Other ways to respond to sustain talk:

Come alongside it: "This change feels too hard right now."

Emphasize autonomy: "You get to decide what makes sense for you."

Shift focus: Don't dwell on the sustain talk. Acknowledge it briefly, then ask about something else.

Teen: "I can't possibly study more. I'm already overwhelmed."

Parent: "You're feeling maxed out already. What would help you feel less overwhelmed?" (Acknowledges concern, shifts to problem-solving)

The goal isn't to eliminate sustain talk. Ambivalence is normal. The goal is to not strengthen it by arguing against it.

5.6 The Screen Time Dialogue

Let's look at a complete dialogue showing how to recognize and respond to both change talk and sustain talk. This builds on Aisha and Layla's conversation from earlier.

Aisha: "Layla, I've been thinking about our screen time conversation. How are you feeling about your phone use lately?"

Layla: "Honestly, I know it's too much." (Change talk: awareness of problem)

Aisha: "You're noticing it's more than you'd like." (Reflection strengthening change talk)

Layla: "Yeah, but like, everyone is always on their phones. It's just how we live now." (Sustain talk: normalizing the behavior)

Aisha: "It feels normal because it's what everyone does." (Reflection, not arguing)

Layla: "Right. So it's not like I'm the only one."

Aisha: "True. And you also mentioned missing drawing." (Acknowledging sustain talk, pivoting to earlier change talk)

Layla: "I do miss it. I used to love drawing. But I never have time." (Change talk: desire)

Aisha: "If you had more time, you'd want to draw again." (Reflection)

Layla: "Definitely. I have so many ideas, I just never actually do them."

Aisha: "What gets in the way?" (Open question)

Layla: "Honestly? My phone. I pick it up to check one thing and then suddenly an hour's gone by." (Change talk: recognizing the problem)

Aisha: "So your phone is eating up time you'd rather spend drawing." (Reflection)

Layla: "Yeah. It's kind of ridiculous actually."

Aisha: "If you could find a way to spend less time on your phone and more time drawing, how would that feel?" (Evocative question)

Layla: "Good. Like I was actually doing something meaningful." (Change talk: reasons for change)

Aisha: "Creating art feels meaningful to you in a way that scrolling doesn't." (Reflection)

Layla: "Exactly."

Aisha: "What ideas do you have about making that happen?" (Open question inviting solutions)

Layla: "I don't know. Maybe I could, like, set a timer or something? Limit myself to 30 minutes at a time?"

Aisha: "That's one approach. What else?" (Affirming her idea, inviting more)

Layla: "I could put my phone in another room while I draw. So I'm not tempted to check it."

Aisha: "So you're thinking about both limiting time and creating physical distance from the phone." (Summary)

Layla: "Yeah. I mean, I know I need to do something. I don't want to look back at high school and realize I spent it all staring at a screen." (Strong change talk: need, reasons)

Aisha: "This really matters to you." (Reflection)

Layla: "It does. I'm going to try the timer thing. Starting tonight."

Notice what Aisha didn't do. She didn't lecture about phone addiction. She didn't create rules or consequences. She didn't argue when Layla defended her phone use. She simply helped Layla explore her own thinking, recognize the conflict between her behavior and her values, and generate her own solutions.

The entire conversation was Layla talking herself into reducing screen time. That's the power of change talk.

5.7 Bringing It Together

Change talk is the language of motivation. When your teen generates change talk, they're building their own case for change. Your job is to recognize it, strengthen it, and gently soften sustain talk without arguing against it.

Listen for DARN CAT. Notice when your teen expresses desire, ability, reasons, need, commitment, activation, or reports taking steps. When you hear these, use reflections and questions to elaborate and strengthen them.

When you hear sustain talk, resist the urge to argue. Reflect it neutrally, then shift focus. Don't dwell on the reasons not to change. Spend your conversational energy on the reasons and resources for change.

This takes practice. You'll catch yourself arguing with sustain talk. You'll miss change talk when it appears. That's normal. Keep practicing. Over time, you'll get better at hearing and responding to the language of change.

The next chapter tackles one of the toughest challenges in parent-teen communication: what to do when you hit resistance and conflict seems inevitable.

Chapter 6.0: Navigating Resistance Without Struggles

"You don't understand!" your teen shouts, slamming their bedroom door. Or they go silent, arms crossed, face closed. Or they argue every single point, turning a simple conversation into an exhausting debate.

This is resistance. And here's the hard truth: when you encounter resistance, it usually means you're doing something wrong.

Not wrong as in you're a bad parent. Wrong as in your approach is triggering your teen's psychological defenses. The good news? Once you understand resistance, you can respond to it in ways that dissolve conflict instead of escalating it.

6.1 Resistance as Feedback

In Motivational Interviewing, resistance isn't something to overcome. It's information. It tells you that your approach isn't working in this moment.

Think of resistance like a dashboard warning light in your car. The light isn't the problem. It's telling you about a problem. You don't fix a car by covering up the warning light. You address what's causing it.

Same with resistance. When your teen resists, they're telling you something. Usually one of these things:

"I feel controlled." You've slipped into directing or pressuring. They're defending their autonomy.

"I don't feel heard." You've jumped to solutions before understanding their perspective.

"This doesn't fit my experience." You're explaining their reality to them instead of listening to their reality.

"I'm not ready." You're moving faster than they can go.

When you understand resistance this way, it changes how you respond. Instead of pushing harder (which creates more resistance), you back off and try a different approach.

Here's what happened with Marcus and his son Andre, 16. Andre had been staying up until 2 or 3 a.m. on school nights. Marcus kept telling him he needed more sleep, citing articles about teenage brain development. Andre kept resisting, saying he wasn't tired, he could function fine, his sleep was his business.

The more Marcus pushed, the later Andre stayed up. Marcus thought he was helping by educating Andre about sleep science. But Andre experienced it as control. Each lecture triggered more resistance.

When Marcus learned to see resistance as feedback, he changed his approach. Instead of pushing harder, he backed off and got curious.

Marcus: "I notice I keep bringing up sleep, and you keep shutting me down. What's that about?"

Andre: "Because you're trying to control me. I'm 16, I can decide when to go to bed."

Marcus: "You're right. It is your decision." (Affirming autonomy)

Andre: (surprised) "Oh. Okay then."

Marcus: "Though I'm curious, what do you notice about how you feel when you get different amounts of sleep?"

This opened a different conversation. By acknowledging the resistance and affirming autonomy, Marcus dissolved the power struggle. Then his question invited Andre to examine his own experience instead of defending against his dad's agenda.

6.2 Roll With Resistance

There's a principle in MI called **rolling with resistance**. Instead of pushing back against resistance, you go with it. Like in martial arts, you use your opponent's force rather than meeting it head-on.

When your teen says something resistant, you have choices:

Option 1: Argue against it. (This strengthens resistance.) **Option 2**: Ignore it. (This feels dismissive.) **Option 3**: Roll with it. (This diffuses it.)

Rolling with resistance means you acknowledge what they said without agreeing or disagreeing, then you shift perspective slightly.

Teen: "You can't make me do my homework!"

Arguing: "Actually, I can. You're grounded until it's done."

Rolling: "You're right. I can't make you. Ultimately, you get to choose what you do. What do you think happens if you don't do it?"

See the difference? Rolling with resistance acknowledges the truth in what they're saying (you can't actually force them to do homework), affirms their autonomy (they do get to choose), then invites them to think through the situation themselves.

Teen: "All my friends are allowed to stay out later than me!"

Arguing: "I don't care what other parents do. In this house, we have rules."

Rolling: "It sounds like our curfew feels unfair compared to what your friends have. Tell me more about that."

You're not agreeing the curfew is unfair. You're acknowledging their feeling and inviting conversation. This defuses the defensiveness and creates space for actual discussion.

Here's how Elena used this with her daughter Sofia, 15, about a party. Sofia wanted to go to a party where Elena knew there would be drinking. When Elena said no, Sofia exploded with resistance.

Sofia: "You're so unfair! You don't trust me! You treat me like a child!"

Elena's instinct was to argue: "This isn't about trust. It's about safety!" But she caught herself and rolled with it instead.

Elena: "It feels really unfair to you, and you're frustrated that I'm setting this limit."

Sofia: "Yes! All my friends are going!"

54

Elena: "So you feel left out and like I'm the only parent being strict about this."

Sofia: "Exactly!"

Elena: "I get why that's frustrating. Help me understand what you're most upset about. Is it missing the party itself, or missing being with your friends, or feeling like I don't trust your judgment?"

Sofia paused, thrown by the question. "I guess... all of it? But mostly I don't want to be the only one who didn't go."

Elena: "The social cost of missing it feels really high."

Sofia: "Yeah."

Elena: "Okay. Let's think about this together. What are your concerns about this party, if you have any?"

By rolling with the resistance instead of arguing against it, Elena opened space for a real conversation. Sofia moved from defensive anger to actually thinking about the situation.

6.3 Reflection Defuses Conflict

The single most powerful tool for handling resistance is simple reflection. When your teen is upset, angry, or resistant, resist the urge to explain, justify, or argue. Just reflect what you're hearing.

This feels weird. Counterintuitive. Your teen is being unreasonable, and you're just... repeating it back? Yes. Because reflection does something magical. It makes people feel heard, which instantly reduces defensiveness.

Teen: "You never let me do anything! My life is basically prison!"

Arguing: "That's ridiculous. You have plenty of freedom."

Reflecting: "You feel like I'm too restrictive and you don't have enough freedom."

Teen: "Yes! Everyone else has way more freedom than me!"

Arguing: "Everyone else's parents are too permissive."

Reflecting: "It seems like other parents allow things I don't allow."

Teen: "Yeah! Like staying out later, or going places without checking in every five seconds."

Reflecting: "So curfew and check-ins are places where you'd like more flexibility."

Notice what happened. By reflecting instead of defending, you moved from a fight to a conversation. Your teen went from general complaining ("You never let me do anything!") to specific issues (curfew, check-ins) that you can actually discuss.

Reflection works because it satisfies the human need to be understood. When people feel heard, they calm down. When they feel unheard, they escalate until someone listens.

Here's what Diego learned about using reflection with his daughter Camila, 14. Camila came home from school furious about a teacher who'd given her detention for being late to class.

Camila: "Mr. Johnson is such a jerk! I was literally 30 seconds late and he gave me detention!"

Diego's first instinct: "Well, you should get to class on time."

What he actually said: "You're really angry about getting detention for being just a little bit late."

Camila: "Yes! And it wasn't even my fault. My locker jammed!"

Diego: "So you had a reason for being late, and you don't think he should have given you detention for something beyond your control."

Camila: "Exactly! He didn't even ask why I was late. He just immediately wrote me up."

Diego: "That feels unfair, not getting a chance to explain."

Camila: "It is unfair!" (Starting to calm down slightly)

Diego: "What are you going to do about the detention?"

Camila: "I have to go. But I'm going to talk to him tomorrow and explain what happened."

By just reflecting Camila's experience without judging or correcting, Diego helped her process her anger and arrive at a constructive plan. If he'd led with "you should get to class on time," they would have fought about whose fault it was instead of dealing with the actual situation.

6.4 Reframing Shifts Perspective

Sometimes resistance comes from how your teen is viewing a situation. **Reframing** means offering a different way to look at it, not to change their mind, but to invite consideration of other perspectives.

Reframing isn't telling them they're wrong. It's offering an alternative frame they might not have considered.

Teen: "You're making me see a therapist. It's like you think I'm broken."

Arguing: "I don't think you're broken. Stop being dramatic."

Reframing: "I wonder if there's another way to look at it. What if therapy isn't about being broken, but about getting support through a tough time? Like how athletes have trainers even when they're not injured."

Teen: "My curfew is all about you controlling me."

Arguing: "It's not about control. It's about safety!"

Reframing: "I can see how it might feel controlling. What if we thought about it differently? What if curfew is less about me controlling you and more about us working out how to balance your growing independence with my responsibility to keep you safe?"

The key to effective reframing is the invitation. You're not telling them how they should view it. You're offering a possibility: "What if we looked at it this way instead?" This respects their autonomy while introducing new information or perspective.

Another powerful reframe is highlighting values instead of rules.

Teen: "This rule is stupid."

Arguing: "The rule stays. Period."

Reframing: "What matters to me is your safety. The specific rule is one way to address that. If you have other ideas for how to handle the safety piece, I'm open to hearing them."

This shifts from "follow my rule because I said so" to "here's what I value, let's figure out how to honor that together."

6.5 The Curfew Showdown

Let's see all these principles in action. This is a scenario almost every parent of teenagers faces.

Background: James is 16. His curfew is 10 p.m. on weeknights, 11 p.m. on weekends. All his friends have later curfews. This has become a constant source of conflict.

James: "Dad, I need to talk to you about my curfew. It's ridiculous. All my friends can stay out until midnight on weekends, at least. Some don't even have curfews."

Old approach (arguing): "I don't care what other parents do. Ten o'clock is reasonable for a 16-year-old. You need sleep. End of discussion."

MI approach:

Dad: "Your curfew feels too early compared to your friends." (Reflection)

James: "Way too early. It's embarrassing. I have to leave parties early, I miss out on stuff. It makes me look like a baby."

Dad: "The social cost is high. You feel like you're missing out and it affects how your friends see you." (Reflection)

James: "Yes! Exactly!"

Dad: "What would feel fair to you?" (Open question, inviting his perspective)

James: "Midnight. At least on weekends."

Dad: "Okay. Midnight on weekends. What's your thinking about why that would work better?" (Evocative question)

James: "Because then I wouldn't have to leave early. I could actually stay for the whole thing, whatever we're doing."

Dad: "So it's really about not having to leave when things are still going on." (Reflection)

James: "Yeah."

Dad: "I get that. Can I share what I'm thinking about?" (Asking permission before sharing perspective)

James: "Sure."

Dad: "I worry about safety, honestly. Not that I don't trust you, but things can happen late at night. Accidents, people making bad decisions, all of that. And I also notice on nights you stay out late, you're exhausted the next day even if it's the weekend." (Sharing concerns without lecturing)

James: "I mean, yeah, but that's my choice, right? To be tired?"

Dad: "It is your choice. And at the same time, I'm still your parent, which means I still have some responsibility for your wellbeing." (Affirming autonomy while maintaining parental role)

James: "So what, we just stick with 10 o'clock forever?"

Dad: "Not necessarily. I'm wondering if there's something that addresses both our concerns. You want more flexibility to stay out with friends. I want to know you're safe and not completely wrecking your sleep schedule. What might work for both of us?" (Reframing as shared problem-solving)

James: (thinking) "What if I could stay out later on nights when I don't have to be anywhere the next morning? Like Friday nights I could have midnight, but Saturday nights back to 11 since I have church Sunday morning?"

Dad: "That's creative. You're thinking about matching curfew to what's happening the next day." (Affirmation)

James: "Yeah. And maybe I could text you when I leave wherever I am, so you know I'm on my way home?"

Dad: "The check-in would help me worry less." (Reflection)

James: "So could we try it? Midnight on Fridays, 11 on Saturdays, 10 on weeknights?"

Dad: "Let's try it for a month and see how it goes. If you're consistently home on time and managing your responsibilities, we'll keep it. If it becomes a problem, we revisit. Fair?" (Provisional agreement with clear terms)

James: "Fair."

Notice what happened. Dad didn't argue about why the old curfew was reasonable. He didn't lecture about safety. He didn't just cave to James's request either. Instead, he used MI skills to create a collaborative conversation where they solved the problem together.

James felt heard. Dad's concerns were addressed. They reached an agreement James helped create, which means he's more likely to honor it.

This is what rolling with resistance looks like in practice.

6.6 Key Takeaways

Resistance isn't your enemy. It's information about your approach. When you encounter it, don't push harder. Back off and try something different.

Roll with resistance by acknowledging it without arguing against it. Use reflection to help your teen feel heard. Reframe situations to invite new perspectives. And most importantly, partner with your teen to solve problems together instead of imposing solutions from above.

This doesn't mean you have no authority or boundaries. It means you exercise that authority in ways that minimize resistance and maximize collaboration.

The next chapter introduces tools for helping your teen recognize gaps between their values and behavior, which creates internal motivation for change without you having to push.

Chapter 7.0: Developing Discrepancy

Your teen values being healthy but eats junk food constantly. They care about their future but blow off homework. They want their parents' trust but keep lying. These contradictions drive parents crazy. Why can't they see the gap between what they say matters and what they actually do?

Here's the thing: they can't see it because you keep pointing it out. Every time you highlight the discrepancy, they defend against it. But when you help them discover it themselves, it creates powerful motivation for change.

This chapter shows you how to develop discrepancy, helping your teen recognize conflicts between their values and their behavior without you doing the pointing.

7.1 Values Drive Behavior

People don't change because of facts or logic. They change when they recognize that their current behavior conflicts with something they care about.

Your teen knows vaping is unhealthy. Lecturing them about health risks won't create change because the knowledge is already there. What creates change is them recognizing that vaping conflicts with values they hold. Maybe they value athletic performance and realize vaping hurts their stamina. Maybe they value honesty and feel guilty lying to you about it. Maybe they value their future and recognize vaping could become a costly addiction.

The specific value matters less than the recognition that their behavior doesn't match what they care about. This internal conflict, this **discrepancy**, is what motivates change.

Your job is to help your teen identify what they value, then help them examine how their choices align or conflict with those values. You're not imposing your values. You're helping them clarify their own.

Here's how Wei's mom helped him recognize discrepancy. Wei, 15, spent hours gaming every day. His grades were dropping, he'd quit soccer, and he seemed increasingly isolated. His mom used to lecture about gaming addiction. It never worked.

Then she learned to explore values first.

Mom: "Wei, what matters to you? When you think about your life, what's important?"

Wei: (shrugging) "I don't know. Friends, I guess. Doing well enough in school to keep my parents off my back."

Mom: "Friends matter. School matters enough that you don't want us nagging. What else?"

Wei: "I want to get into a decent college. Go somewhere good."

Mom: "College is important to you. What would a 'good' college give you?"

Wei: "I don't know. Good job eventually? Not living in my parents' basement when I'm 30?" (Half joking)

Mom: "So independence matters. Your own life, your own success."

Wei: "Yeah, I guess."

Mom: "How do you see gaming fitting with those things you value? Friends, college, future independence?"

Wei: (pause) "I mean... it doesn't really, does it? My gaming friends aren't real friends. And it's definitely not helping my grades."

Notice what Mom didn't do. She didn't tell Wei that gaming was ruining his life. She helped him articulate his values, then invited him to examine the fit. Wei identified the discrepancy himself.

7.2 Exploring Consequences Gently

Teenagers know there are consequences to their choices. Lecturing about consequences doesn't help because it triggers their righting reflex (remember section 1.4?). They defend against your dire warnings instead of actually thinking about what might happen.

But you can invite them to explore consequences themselves through questions.

Instead of: "If you keep skipping class, you're going to fail!"

Try: "What do you think happens if you keep missing classes? How would that play out?"

Instead of: "Staying out all night is going to get you in serious trouble!"

Try: "Walk me through what you think happens after you stay out all night. What's the likely outcome?"

You're not warning or threatening. You're inviting them to think through the natural trajectory of their choices.

Here's how this worked for Priya and her daughter Ananya, 16. Ananya wanted to quit the debate team mid-season to hang out with a new boyfriend.

Old approach: "You made a commitment! You can't just quit because a boy came along! You'll regret this!"

New approach:

Priya: "You're thinking about quitting debate. Walk me through what happens if you do that."

Ananya: "I just... I'd have more free time. I could see Marcus more."

Priya: "Okay. More time with Marcus. What else happens?"

Ananya: "I mean, the team would be annoyed. Coach would be mad."

Priya: "How would that feel for you?"

Ananya: "Not great, I guess. They've been counting on me."

Priya: "What about the college application piece? You were planning to highlight debate."

Ananya: "Oh. Yeah. I don't know. I could just not mention it?"

Priya: "How would you feel about that?"

Ananya: (pause) "Kind of lame actually. Like I gave up something I was good at."

Priya: "So there's a cost beyond just quitting the team. It affects how you see yourself."

Ananya: "I really like Marcus though."

Priya: "I hear that. What if you finished the season and then had more time after? How would that work?"

Ananya: "That's like three more months."

Priya: "It is. What would Marcus think about you finishing what you started?"

Ananya: (thinking) "Honestly? He'd probably respect it. He's not the type to want me to quit stuff for him."

By exploring consequences through questions rather than warnings, Priya helped Ananya think through the decision. Ananya identified the costs herself, which carried much more weight than her mom's lectures would have.

7.3 The Decisional Balance

A powerful tool for developing discrepancy is the **decisional balance**. This helps your teen examine both sides of a decision by listing out the pros and cons of changing versus staying the same.

You can do this conversationally or actually write it out. The key is exploring all four quadrants:

1. Benefits of changing
2. Costs of changing
3. Benefits of staying the same
4. Costs of staying the same

Most teens (and adults) only think about quadrants 1 and 3. They know there would be benefits to change, but there are also benefits to keeping things as they are. This keeps them stuck.

Quadrants 2 and 4 are where the action happens. What would it cost to change? What's it costing to stay the same? When teens recognize the true cost of not changing, motivation shifts.

Here's how Carlos used this with his son Miguel, 17, about his drinking.

Carlos: "Miguel, I want to understand your thinking about drinking. Can we talk through it?"

Miguel: (wary) "I guess."

Carlos: "What do you get out of drinking? What are the benefits for you?"

Miguel: "I don't know. It's fun. I feel more relaxed. Everyone else is doing it."

Carlos: "So it helps you relax and feel part of the group. What else?"

Miguel: "That's pretty much it."

Carlos: "Okay. Now, what are the downsides? What does drinking cost you?"

Miguel: "I mean, you guys get mad. And sometimes I feel like crap the next day."

Carlos: "Mad parents, hangovers. What else?"

Miguel: "I worry sometimes. Like, what if I get in an accident or something stupid happens?"

Carlos: "So there's some anxiety about risk."

Miguel: "Yeah."

Carlos: "Now let's flip it. If you stopped drinking or drank less, what would be the benefits?"

Miguel: "You and Mom would get off my back. I wouldn't feel sick on Saturdays. Maybe my running would get better, Coach says alcohol affects performance."

Carlos: "So better relationship with us, feeling better physically, improved running. What else?"

Miguel: "I guess I wouldn't worry as much. Like, I could just go out and not have to think about getting caught or something bad happening."

Carlos: "Less anxiety. And what would be the downside of drinking less or stopping?"

Miguel: "My friends would think I'm lame. I'd feel left out at parties."

Carlos: "So there's a real social cost. That matters."

Miguel: "Yeah, it does."

Carlos: "Looking at all of this, what stands out to you?"

Miguel: (thinking) "I guess... the reasons to drink are mostly about other people. Fitting in, being part of the group. But the reasons not to drink are more about me. My health, my running, not being stressed."

Notice how Carlos didn't argue for quitting drinking. He helped Miguel examine all four quadrants, then asked what stood out. Miguel came to his own realization about what mattered more.

7.4 The Importance Ruler

Another useful tool is the **importance ruler**. You ask your teen to rate how important a change is to them on a scale of 1 to 10. Then you ask strategic follow-up questions.

The magic isn't in the number they give. It's in the questions that follow.

Parent: "On a scale of 1 to 10, where 10 is extremely important and 1 is not important at all, how important is it to you to bring up your math grade?"

Teen: "I don't know. Maybe a 6?"

Parent: "A 6. What makes it a 6 and not a 2?" (This invites change talk about why it matters)

Teen: "Because I know I need math for college. And my grade is pretty bad right now."

Parent: "So it matters for your future, and you're concerned about where it is now. What would it take to make it an 8?" (This invites them to think about moving toward more importance)

Teen: "I guess if I felt like I could actually improve it. Right now it feels hopeless."

See what happened? The number itself (6) wasn't that meaningful. But the questions around it helped the teen articulate why change matters and what's in the way.

The importance ruler works because it:

- Acknowledges ambivalence (a 6 means yes and no)
- Elicits change talk ("what makes it a 6 and not a 2?")
- Identifies barriers ("what would make it an 8?")
- Keeps it conversational, not confrontational

You can also use a **confidence ruler** to explore capability.

Parent: "On a scale of 1 to 10, how confident are you that you could cut your screen time in half if you decided to?"

Teen: "Maybe a 4?"

Parent: "A 4. What makes you think you could do it at all? Why not a 0?" (Eliciting self-efficacy)

Teen: "I mean, I've done it before when I was busy with other stuff. Like during soccer season I didn't use my phone as much."

Parent: "So you know you're capable when you're focused on something else. What would help you get to a 6 or 7?" (Building on capability, problem-solving)

These rulers are simple but powerful tools for developing discrepancy and exploring both importance and capability.

7.5 Values Clarification Exercise

Let's make this practical with an exercise you can do with your teen.

Step 1: Together, brainstorm a list of values that might matter to them. Don't judge what they include. Just generate a list.

Examples: friendship, honesty, independence, achievement, creativity, family, health, fun, kindness, respect, freedom, success, learning, adventure, helping others, faith, authenticity

Step 2: Ask them to pick their top five values. What matters most to them right now in their life?

Step 3: For each value, ask: "On a scale of 1 to 10, how much is your life right now reflecting this value?"

This is where it gets interesting. They might say independence is a top value but rate their current life a 3 for independence. That gap creates motivation.

Step 4: For any value where there's a gap, ask: "What would it take to move that number higher? What would be different if this value was more present in your life?"

Step 5: Connect to specific behaviors or choices. "How does [behavior you're concerned about] fit with [their stated value]?"

Example: "You said honesty is one of your top values. How does lying about where you're going fit with that?"

You're not lecturing. You're helping them examine the discrepancy.

Here's how this played out for Jennifer and her son David, 15.

They did the values exercise together. David's top five were: friendship, independence, achievement, fun, respect.

For independence, he rated his current life a 4 out of 10. "I feel like I have no control over anything. You guys control my schedule, my screen time, everything."

Jennifer resisted the urge to defend. Instead, she asked, "What would have to change for that number to be higher?"

David: "If I had more say in things. If you trusted me to make decisions."

Jennifer: "That makes sense. What decisions feel most important to have say in?"

David: "How I spend my free time. When I hang out with friends. Stuff like that."

Jennifer: "Okay. Let's think about that. How does your lying about where you're going fit with getting more independence?"

David: (pause) "I guess it doesn't. If I want you to trust me, lying doesn't help."

Jennifer: "Right. And you also said respect was a top value. Tell me about that."

David: "I want people to respect me. Not treat me like a kid."

Jennifer: "How do you earn respect?"

David: (thinking) "By being responsible. By doing what you say you'll do."

Jennifer: "How's that going right now?"

David: "Not great, honestly. I've been kind of flaking on stuff."

Jennifer: "So there's a gap between what you value (respect, independence) and how you've been acting (lying, flaking). What do you want to do about that?"

Through this conversation, David recognized the discrepancy himself. His behavior wasn't matching his values. That recognition created motivation to change, not because his mom told him to, but because he wanted to live according to what mattered to him.

7.6 What This Means

Developing discrepancy is about helping your teen see gaps between their values and their behavior. You can't force this awareness. You can only invite it through strategic questions, reflections, and tools like decisional balance and importance rulers.

When teens recognize these gaps themselves, they develop internal motivation to change. Not because you nagged or threatened, but because they want to align their life with what matters to them.

The tools in this chapter work best when combined with OARS from Chapter 4.0 and the change talk strategies from Chapter 5.0. Everything builds on everything else.

You now have a comprehensive toolkit for Motivational Interviewing with your teen. The remaining chapters show you how to apply these skills to specific situations like screen time, academics, substance use, and other common challenges.

Chapter 8.0: The Screen Time Struggle

"Put your phone away!" "Just one more minute!" "I said NOW!" Sound familiar? If you've had this exact exchange 47 times this week, welcome to the screen time struggle that's consuming families everywhere.

Here's the frustrating part. You know excessive screen time isn't good for your teen. The research backs you up. But every attempt to set limits turns into World War III. Your teen acts like you're asking them to cut off their right arm. And honestly? Maybe you're starting to wonder if you're being too strict.

This chapter shows you how to use MI to address screen time without the constant battles, helping your teen recognize the impact themselves and develop their own motivation to change.

8.1 Why Limits Create Struggles

Screen time is different from other parenting challenges. It's not like curfew or homework, issues that have existed for generations. Smartphones and social media tap into something primal in the teenage brain: social connection, novelty, and instant rewards.

Remember from section 1.1, the teenage limbic system is hypersensitive to rewards. Every notification, like, comment, and message triggers a dopamine hit. Meanwhile, the underdeveloped prefrontal cortex struggles to override this pull with long-term thinking. Your teen literally feels compelled to check their phone, and their brain isn't great at resisting that compulsion.

When you impose screen limits, you're fighting their neurobiology plus their social world. Their friends are online. Missing group chats means missing out on plans, inside jokes, social currency. To you, it's just reducing phone time. To them, it feels like social exile.

This is why traditional limit-setting backfires. You set a rule: one hour of phone time per day. They agree (or don't, but they have no choice). Then they break it. You take the phone away. They're furious, you're frustrated, and nothing actually changes about their relationship with screens.

The power struggle happens because limits feel controlling. As we discussed in section 3.3, teens need autonomy. Arbitrary rules imposed from above trigger resistance. And screen time rules often feel arbitrary to teens because we're not helping them understand the "why" in a way that resonates with their experience.

Here's what happened with the Martinez family. Elena's daughter Camila, 14, was on her phone constantly. Elena tried everything. Screen time limits through the phone settings. Camila found workarounds. Taking the phone at night. Camila stayed up late on her laptop instead. Threatening consequences. Camila complied minimally but resentfully.

The more Elena tried to control Camila's screen use, the more Camila resisted. It became the defining conflict in their relationship. Neither of them was happy. And Camila's screen time? Didn't actually decrease.

8.2 Exploring Impact Together

Instead of imposing limits and hoping your teen complies, MI invites you to explore the impact of screen time together. You're not telling them it's bad. You're helping them examine how it affects things they care about.

This starts with genuine curiosity. What do they get from screen time? How does it make them feel? What would be different if they used screens less? What do they notice about themselves when they're on screens a lot versus very little?

These questions aren't rhetorical. You genuinely want to know their experience. Because until they recognize the costs themselves, your lectures about screen addiction will fall on deaf ears.

Here's how to explore impact using the skills from Chapters 4.0 through 7.0:

Use open questions to understand their perspective:

- "What do you like about being on your phone so much?"
- "How do you feel after spending several hours scrolling?"
- "What do you notice about your sleep on nights when you're on your phone late?"

Reflect what you hear without judgment:

- "So TikTok helps you relax after a stressful day."
- "You worry that if you're not on the group chat, you'll miss important plans."
- "You've noticed you feel kind of empty after scrolling for hours, but in the moment it's hard to stop."

Affirm their self-awareness:

- "You're paying attention to how screen time affects you. That's insightful."
- "It takes courage to admit that it's become a problem even though your friends don't see it that way."

Develop discrepancy by connecting to their values (remember section 7.1):

- "You mentioned wanting to make the basketball team. How does staying up until 2 a.m. on your phone fit with that goal?"
- "You said you value real friendships. What's the difference between connection online versus in person?"

This exploration is not a one-time conversation. It's an ongoing dialogue where you help your teen notice patterns, recognize costs, and identify what matters to them.

8.3 The Gaming Concern Dialogue

Let's look at a complete conversation using MI to address gaming concerns. This builds on the skills we've developed in previous chapters.

Background: Marcus's son Andre, 16, plays video games from the moment he gets home until midnight or later. His grades have dropped. He quit soccer. He seems isolated from real-world friends. Marcus is worried but previous attempts to limit gaming have led to massive fights.

Marcus decides to try an MI approach.

Marcus: "Andre, I want to talk about gaming. Not to lecture you or set new rules right now. I'm genuinely trying to understand what's going on for you. Is now okay?" (Asking permission, setting collaborative tone)

Andre: (wary) "I guess."

Marcus: "How many hours do you think you're gaming on a typical day?"

Andre: "I don't know. Maybe three or four hours?"

Marcus: "Okay. What do you love about it?" (Open question, starting with the positives)

Andre: "It's fun. I'm good at it. And my friends are online. We play together."

Marcus: "So it's enjoyable, you have skill at it, and it's social." (Reflection)

Andre: "Yeah, exactly."

Marcus: "What else is good about gaming for you?"

Andre: "I don't know. It's relaxing, I guess. Like I can just zone out and not think about school or whatever."

Marcus: "It gives you an escape from stress." (Reflection)

Andre: "Yeah."

Marcus: "I'm curious about something. You used to love soccer. What happened with that?" (Open question, exploring what changed)

Andre: (shrugs) "I just didn't feel like it anymore."

Marcus: "Was there a specific reason, or did you just lose interest?" (Following up gently)

Andre: "I mean, practice was after school, which is when I wanted to game. And I was tired from staying up late. So I'd have a bad practice, and it stopped being fun."

Marcus: "So gaming was interfering with soccer, and then soccer started feeling like a chore instead of something you enjoyed." (Reflection showing the connection)

Andre: "I guess, yeah."

Marcus: "Do you miss soccer at all?"

Andre: (pause) "Sometimes. I miss being good at something in real life, not just online."

Marcus: "That's interesting. Say more about that, the difference between being good online versus in real life." (Inviting elaboration on change talk)

Andre: "I don't know. Gaming is fun, but it's not real, you know? Like, I could be the best player in the world at this game, and it wouldn't actually matter. With soccer, I was good at something that mattered. Colleges care about that. My body was in better shape. I had actual friends, not just online ones."

Marcus: "So there are some real costs to gaming taking over. You lost something that gave you a different kind of satisfaction." (Reflection highlighting discrepancy)

Andre: "Yeah. But I don't want to quit gaming completely. That's not realistic."

Marcus: "Nobody's saying you have to quit. I'm just trying to understand what you notice about the balance right now." (Affirming autonomy, rolling with resistance)

Andre: "The balance sucks, honestly. I know I game too much."

Marcus: "You recognize it's more than you'd like it to be." (Reflection of change talk)

Andre: "Yeah. But I don't know how to stop. Like, I try to get off earlier, but then one more match turns into three more matches."

Marcus: "It's hard to stop once you start." (Reflection)

Andre: "Exactly."

Marcus: "If you could find a way to game less and maybe get back into other stuff, what would that look like?" (Evocative question)

Andre: "I don't know. Maybe limit myself to two hours on weeknights? And I've been thinking about trying out for the spring soccer season."

Marcus: "Those are concrete ideas. What would help you actually follow through?" (Open question moving toward planning)

Notice what Marcus didn't do. He didn't lecture about gaming addiction. He didn't impose limits. He didn't argue when Andre said he didn't want to quit completely. Instead, he helped Andre recognize the costs himself and generate his own ideas for change.

8.4 Creating Collaborative Agreements

Once your teen has recognized that screen time is affecting things they care about (using discrepancy from section 7.1), you can move toward creating agreements together. The key word is together.

Traditional approach: "From now on, you're allowed one hour of screen time per day. No exceptions."

Collaborative approach: "You've noticed screen time is getting in the way of things you value. What would a reasonable limit look like to you? What would work for your life?"

The **collaborative screen agreement** has several key elements:

1. **Your teen's input is genuine**. You're not pretending to collaborate while actually imposing your pre-decided rules. You're truly open to their ideas.
2. **It addresses their concerns and yours**. Maybe you're worried about sleep. Maybe they're worried about missing social connections. A good agreement honors both.
3. **It's specific and measurable**. Not "less screen time" but "phone off by 10 p.m. on school nights" or "two hours max on weekdays."
4. **It includes how you'll both know if it's working**. What are the markers of success?
5. **It's provisional**. You'll try it for a set period (two weeks, a month) and then revisit.

Here's what a collaborative agreement process might look like:

Parent: "So you've said you want to cut back on screen time. What feels realistic to you?"

Teen: "Maybe two hours on school nights?"

Parent: "Okay, two hours. How would you track that?"

Teen: "I could use the screen time thing on my phone."

Parent: "And what about right before bed? You mentioned sleep has been an issue."

Teen: "I could put my phone in the kitchen by 10."

Parent: "That could work. What if there's a legit reason you need it later, like a group project thing?"

Teen: "We could have a rule where I ask first?"

Parent: "Okay. So the agreement is: two hours on school nights, tracked on your phone. Device in the kitchen by 10 unless there's a specific reason and you check with me first. Let's try that for two weeks and see how it goes. If it's not working, we'll adjust."

Notice the collaborative language. "What feels realistic?" "How would you track?" "What if?" You're problem-solving together, not dictating.

8.5 When Agreements Break

Your teen will break the agreement. Not maybe. Will. Because change is hard, habits are strong, and teenagers are still developing self-regulation.

Traditional response: "You broke the agreement! That's it, I'm taking your phone for a week!"

MI response: Treat the breakdown as information and an opportunity for problem-solving.

When the agreement breaks, use it as a chance to understand what got in the way. Not in an accusatory way. Genuinely curious.

"I noticed you were on your phone past 10 last night. What happened?"

"You went over two hours yesterday. Tell me about that."

Then listen. Really listen. Maybe they had a bad day and needed the escape. Maybe the time limits aren't realistic. Maybe they don't have other coping strategies for stress. This is all useful information.

Here's how Chen handled it when his daughter Mei broke their screen time agreement three nights in a row.

Chen: "Mei, we agreed on phone in the kitchen by 10, but I've noticed it's been in your room the last few nights. What's going on?" (Observation without accusation)

Mei: "I'm sorry. I just can't fall asleep without scrolling."

Chen: "You need the phone to wind down." (Reflection)

Mei: "Yeah. My brain is too busy otherwise."

Chen: "Okay, so the agreement isn't working because it's interfering with your sleep routine." (Reframing the problem)

Mei: "I guess."

Chen: "Let's think about this differently. What if the goal isn't just getting the phone out of your room, but finding a way for you to wind down that doesn't involve screens? What else might help?" (Shifting to collaborative problem-solving)

Mei: "I don't know. Maybe I could read?"

Chen: "That's one option. What else?"

Mei: "I used to journal sometimes. That was kind of relaxing."

Chen: "So reading or journaling. What would you need to make that happen?"

This conversation didn't result in consequences for breaking the agreement. It resulted in understanding the function the phone was serving (helping her wind down) and problem-solving alternatives.

If agreements consistently break, you need to revisit them. Maybe they're not realistic. Maybe your teen isn't actually committed to changing. Maybe there are barriers you haven't addressed.

Use the importance and confidence rulers from section 7.4:

"On a scale of 1 to 10, how important is it to you to reduce screen time?"

"On a scale of 1 to 10, how confident are you that you can stick to this agreement?"

Low importance means you need to spend more time developing discrepancy. Low confidence means you need to problem-solve obstacles.

8.6 Digital Wellness Resources

Sometimes teens need more support than family agreements can provide. If screen use is severely impacting daily functioning, consider additional resources.

Signs that professional help might be needed:

- Complete withdrawal from in-person relationships
- Severe sleep disruption affecting health or safety
- Academic failure directly tied to screen use
- Using screens to cope with serious mental health issues
- Continuing heavy use despite significant negative consequences

Resources worth exploring include:

- Therapists who specialize in adolescent technology use
- Apps designed to help with phone addiction that use motivational strategies
- Support groups for families dealing with gaming or social media concerns

When considering professional help, frame it collaboratively:

"I'm noticing screen time is really affecting your life in ways that worry both of us. What do you think about talking to someone who specializes in helping teens figure out a healthier balance?"

Not: "You're addicted. You need therapy."

The MI approach applies here too. Help your teen recognize they might benefit from support, rather than forcing them into it.

8.7 Moving Forward

Screen time is one of the most challenging issues for modern parents. You can't completely eliminate screens (nor should you). They're part of how your teen connects, learns, and navigates their world. But you can help your teen develop a healthier relationship with technology.

Using MI means you're partnering with your teen to explore impact, develop their own motivation to change, and create collaborative solutions. It's slower than just setting rules. But it's also more likely to actually work.

The next chapter applies these same MI principles to another common battleground: homework and grades.

Chapter 9.0: Homework and Academic Motivation

Your teen has a test tomorrow. They haven't studied. You know this. They know you know. And here comes the nightly battle about homework that you're both so tired of having.

The homework struggle is exhausting for everyone. You want them to succeed. They want you off their back. You nag, they resist. Grades slip, anxiety rises, and somewhere along the way, the actual learning gets lost.

This chapter shows you how to step back from the homework police role and help your teen develop their own academic motivation.

9.1 The Autonomy Paradox

Here's the paradox parents face with homework. The more you manage it, the less your teen develops self-management skills. But if you don't manage it, they fail. So you feel stuck micromanaging something that should be their responsibility.

This is what happened with the Johnson family. Their son Tyler, 15, would not do homework without constant supervision. Mom sat with him every night, prompting him to focus, reminding him of deadlines, checking every answer. It was exhausting. When she tried to step back, his grades plummeted.

Tyler had no intrinsic motivation for homework because Mom handled all the external management. He didn't track assignments because Mom tracked them. He didn't experience natural consequences because Mom prevented them. At 15, he functioned like a much younger child academically, not because he wasn't capable, but because the scaffolding had never been removed.

The **autonomy paradox** is this: your involvement prevents the very independence you're trying to create. But stepping back completely feels irresponsible.

MI offers a middle path. You don't abandon your teen to sink or swim. But you shift from managing their homework to helping them develop the skills to manage it themselves.

This means:

- Asking instead of telling
- Supporting instead of doing
- Letting natural consequences teach (within reason)
- Focusing on the process, not just the grades

9.2 Separating Your Anxiety

Your teen's grades trigger your anxiety. You know academic performance affects college options, future opportunities, their whole life trajectory. When they blow off homework, you catastrophize: they'll fail out, never get into college, end up living in your basement at 35.

Your anxiety is understandable. But when you parent from that anxiety, you make everything worse.

Here's what anxiety-driven parenting looks like:

- "If you don't do this homework, you're going to fail!"
- "Do you want to work at McDonald's your whole life?"
- "I'm not paying for college if you can't even get decent grades!"

These statements come from fear. And they trigger your teen's defenses, not their motivation.

Your teen's academic performance is ultimately their responsibility, not yours. You can support, provide resources, and set reasonable expectations. But you can't make them care more than they do. And your anxiety doesn't help them care more. It just creates pressure they resist.

Here's how to separate your anxiety from their responsibility:

Recognize whose problem it is. If they're failing, it's primarily their problem. You care about it, but it's not happening to you.

Notice your catastrophizing. When you find yourself spiraling about their future, step back. They're not going to be homeless because they got a C in biology.

Focus on what you control. You control whether you create a supportive home environment. You don't control whether they choose to study.

Get your own support. If their academic struggles trigger intense anxiety, talk to a friend, partner, or therapist. Don't make your teen responsible for managing your feelings.

Isabella learned this when her daughter Sofia, 14, stopped turning in assignments. Isabella's anxiety was through the roof. Every missing assignment felt like Sofia was ruining her future. Isabella nagged, pleaded, threatened. Nothing worked.

Then Isabella realized her anxiety was making things worse. Sofia wasn't thinking about her assignments at all. She was thinking about how to avoid her mom's lectures. Isabella's anxiety had become the focus instead of Sofia's academics.

Isabella started managing her own anxiety elsewhere. She journaled, talked to friends, reminded herself that Sofia's grades were Sofia's responsibility. When she stopped bringing panicked energy to homework conversations, Sofia actually started engaging with the issue.

9.3 MI for Unmotivated Students

So how do you help an unmotivated teen without nagging, threatening, or taking over?

You use MI to help them examine their own thinking about school, identify what matters to them, and recognize the gap between their current behavior and their goals.

Start by understanding their perspective: "What's going on with homework lately? Tell me what it's like from your side."

Listen to their actual experience. Maybe they're overwhelmed and don't know where to start. Maybe they don't see the point of assignments they find meaningless. Maybe they're struggling with the material and feel stupid. Maybe they have undiagnosed learning challenges.

You can't address the real issue until you understand it.

Explore values and goals: "When you think about your future, what matters to you?" "What kind of life do you want after high school?" "Where do you see yourself in five years?"

Most teens have some vision for their future, even if vague. Maybe they want to go to college. Maybe they want a specific career. Maybe they just want independence and financial security. These are leverage points for motivation.

Develop discrepancy (remember section 7.1): "You mentioned wanting to go to college. How do your current grades fit with that goal?" "You said independence matters to you. What role does education play in being able to support yourself?"

You're not lecturing about why school matters. You're helping them connect their current choices to their own stated values.

Explore obstacles: "What gets in the way of doing homework?" "What would make it easier?" "When you do manage to get homework done, what's different?"

This isn't interrogation. It's genuine problem-solving. Maybe they need a quieter space. Maybe they're overwhelmed and need help breaking tasks into smaller steps. Maybe they need to address phone distractions. Maybe they need a tutor.

Build on past success: "Was there ever a time when school went better for you? What was different then?"

This helps them recognize they have capability and identify what conditions support their success.

9.4 The Failing Grade Conversation

Let's see MI in action with a specific scenario: your teen brings home a failing grade.

Background: Marcus's son Jamal, 15, has been getting Ds and Fs in English all semester. Report cards just came out with an F for the quarter. Marcus is frustrated and worried.

Old approach: "An F? Are you kidding me? That's unacceptable. You're grounded until you bring this grade up. No phone, no friends, nothing but school and homework."

MI approach:

Marcus: "I saw your English grade. I'm curious how you feel about it." (Open question about their perspective)

Jamal: (defensive) "It's not my fault. The teacher doesn't like me. And the assignments are stupid."

Marcus: "You feel like the teacher is unfair and the work isn't worthwhile." (Reflection, not agreeing or disagreeing)

Jamal: "Yeah."

Marcus: "Tell me more about that. What makes you think the teacher doesn't like you?" (Getting curious instead of arguing)

Jamal: "She's always picking on me about late work. And she gave me a bad grade on my essay when other people wrote worse ones."

Marcus: "So it feels inconsistent and personal." (Reflection)

Jamal: "Yeah."

Marcus: "That sounds frustrating. What about the assignments being stupid? Say more about that." (Exploring without judgment)

Jamal: "Like, why do I need to analyze Shakespeare? I'm never going to use that in real life."

Marcus: "You don't see the point of the material." (Reflection)

Jamal: "No."

Marcus: "I get that. A lot of school feels irrelevant when you're in the middle of it. Can I ask you something though? Regardless of how you feel about the teacher or the assignments, how do you feel about having an F?" (Pivoting to focus on the outcome)

Jamal: (pause) "Not great, honestly."

Marcus: "Say more." (Inviting elaboration)

Jamal: "I mean, I don't want to fail. I know it matters for college and stuff. I just... I don't know how to fix it at this point."

85

Marcus: "So there's a disconnect. You care about passing, but you're not sure how to turn it around." (Reflection identifying the conflict)

Jamal: "Yeah."

Marcus: "What would you need to pass the class?" (Open question shifting to problem-solving)

Jamal: "I don't know. Turn in all my late work, I guess. Do better on the next essay."

Marcus: "Those are concrete steps. What's stopping you from doing that?" (Exploring obstacles)

Jamal: "The late work is overwhelming. There's so much of it."

Marcus: "It feels like too much to tackle." (Reflection)

Jamal: "Yeah."

Marcus: "What if you broke it down? Like, what if you turned in two assignments a week until you're caught up?" (Offering a suggestion as a question, not a directive)

Jamal: "Maybe. That might work."

Marcus: "What support would help you actually do that?" (Identifying needed resources)

Jamal: "Could you help me figure out which assignments to prioritize? And maybe check in with me once a week to make sure I'm doing it?"

Marcus: "I can do that. So the plan is: you tackle two late assignments a week, we look at priorities together, and I check in weekly to see how it's going. Not to nag, just to support. How does that sound?" (Summarizing the collaborative plan)

Jamal: "Okay. I can try that."

Notice what Marcus did. He didn't punish, lecture, or take over. He helped Jamal examine his own thinking, recognize the problem mattered to him, identify concrete steps, and request the support he needed. Jamal is now more likely to follow through because it's his plan, not his dad's.

9.5 When to Step In

So when do you step back and let natural consequences teach, and when do you intervene?

Let natural consequences teach when:

- The stakes are educational, not catastrophic
- Your teen has the capability to succeed if they apply themselves
- The consequence is directly related to their choice
- They're old enough to learn from the experience

Example: They forgot to study for a quiz. Let them take the bad grade and learn from it.

Step in when:

- There are underlying issues (learning disabilities, mental health, bullying) affecting performance
- The consequences are disproportionate or long-lasting
- They genuinely don't have the skills or resources to succeed
- They're drowning and need scaffolding before they can be independent

Example: They're failing because they have undiagnosed ADHD and can't organize assignments. Get them evaluated and provide appropriate support.

The key is differentiating between won't (lack of motivation) and can't (lack of capability). For won't, natural consequences and MI work well. For can't, they need actual help, not just motivation.

Here's how to tell the difference. Ask yourself:

- Do they know HOW to do this task?
- Do they have the executive function skills to manage it?
- Are there obstacles beyond their control?
- Have they ever been successful at this type of thing?

If the answer to these is no, they need support, not consequences.

9.6 Supporting Different Learning Styles

Some homework struggles come from a mismatch between how school teaches and how your teen learns. MI can help you explore this with them.

"What classes go better for you? What's different about those?"

"When do you feel most engaged in learning? What's happening then?"

"What helps you understand new material? Doing it, seeing it, hearing it explained?"

Maybe they're a hands-on learner stuck in lecture-based classes. Maybe they're creative but school rewards analytical thinking. Maybe they're bright but process information more slowly than the pace of class.

Understanding their learning style doesn't mean making excuses. It means helping them develop strategies that work with their brain, not against it.

"You said you learn better by doing than by reading. How could you apply that to studying for history tests?"

"You mentioned you get overwhelmed by long assignments. What if you broke them into 15-minute chunks with breaks in between?"

You're not solving the problem for them. You're helping them become self-aware about their learning needs and develop their own accommodations.

9.7 Essential Points

Homework battles drain everyone and rarely improve academic performance. Using MI means stepping back from the homework police role and helping your teen develop internal motivation and self-management skills.

Separate your anxiety from their responsibility. Their grades are ultimately their problem to solve. You can support without taking over.

Use MI to explore their perspective, identify their values and goals, develop discrepancy between current behavior and future aspirations, and collaboratively problem-solve obstacles.

Know when to let natural consequences teach and when to intervene with support. Some struggles are motivational. Others signal genuine need for help.

The next chapter addresses one of parents' biggest fears: substance use.

Chapter 10.0: Substance Use Conversations

You find a vape in their backpack. Or smell alcohol on their breath. Or discover they've been smoking marijuana with friends. Your heart drops. Fear floods in. And suddenly you're faced with a conversation you hoped you'd never have to have.

Most parents respond with panic-driven lectures. Statistics about addiction. Threats about consequences. Demands that it never happen again. This approach feels necessary because the stakes are so high. But it rarely works.

This chapter shows you how to have honest conversations about substance use that keep the door open, build trust, and actually influence your teen's choices.

10.1 The Honest Talk They Need

Your teen already knows drugs and alcohol can be harmful. They've sat through D.A.R.E. programs and health class. They've seen the scary videos. Lecturing them with more facts won't change their behavior.

What teens need is a conversation, not a lecture. A chance to think through their choices in a safe space. An opportunity to examine their own reasons, concerns, and motivations without being shamed or punished into silence.

The challenge is having this conversation when you're scared. Fear makes us reactive. We want to prevent the worst-case scenario, so we come down hard. Zero tolerance. Harsh consequences. Dire warnings.

But harsh responses drive the behavior underground. Your teen learns to hide it better, not to stop doing it. They stop coming to you when things get dangerous because they fear your reaction more than the risk itself.

Here's what happened with the Peterson family. Their daughter Zoe, 16, came home drunk from a party. Her dad exploded. Grounded her for two months. Threatened to call all her friends' parents. Lectured for an hour about how disappointed he was.

Six months later, Zoe was at another party where someone was dangerously drunk. Zoe wanted to call her parents for help. But she didn't, because she feared their reaction. The friend ended up in the hospital. Zoe felt guilty and alone, but still couldn't talk to her parents about it.

Her dad's harsh response to the first incident ensured Zoe would never come to him again. His fear-driven reaction prioritized punishment over connection. And it made his daughter less safe, not more.

10.2 Harm Reduction Thinking

There are two basic approaches to teen substance use: **zero tolerance** and **harm reduction**.

Zero tolerance says: no substance use, period. Any use results in consequences. The goal is complete abstinence.

Harm reduction says: while abstinence is ideal, if teens choose to use substances, let's minimize the harm. The goal is safety.

Most parents instinctively lean toward zero tolerance. It feels like the responsible position. Harm reduction can feel like you're condoning use.

But here's reality. Some teens will experiment with substances regardless of what you say. Studies show that by 12th grade, roughly two-thirds of teens have tried alcohol and nearly half have tried marijuana. Pretending your teen will definitely abstain might make you feel better, but it doesn't match reality.

Harm reduction doesn't mean you approve of substance use. It means you prioritize your teen's safety and keep communication open, even about choices you wish they wouldn't make.

A zero-tolerance conversation sounds like: "If I ever find out you've been drinking, you're grounded for six months. No exceptions."

A harm-reduction conversation sounds like: "I hope you choose not to drink. But if you ever find yourself in a situation where you or your friends have been drinking, I want you to call me, no matter what. I'll come get you, no questions asked, no punishment. Your safety matters more than rules."

Which approach is more likely to result in your teen calling you when they need help?

Harm reduction strategies include:

- Teaching them to never leave a drink unattended
- Making sure they're with trusted friends
- Having a code word they can text if they need extraction from a bad situation
- Ensuring they know not to mix substances
- Making it clear they can always call for help without fear of punishment

You can maintain your preference for abstinence while also being realistic about risk reduction.

10.3 Using MI to Explore

When you discover substance use, or when you want to have a preventive conversation, MI gives you a framework for discussing it without alienating your teen.

Remember, MI is about helping your teen examine their own thinking, not imposing yours. This is especially important with substance use because shaming and lecturing trigger defensiveness that shuts down real conversation.

Start by understanding their experience: "I want to understand what's going on with vaping. Can you tell me about it?"

Not: "How could you be so stupid?"

Get genuinely curious about their reasons: "What do you like about it?" "What does it do for you?" "How did you get started?"

Your teen has reasons for their choices. Understanding those reasons doesn't mean you agree. It means you're treating them like a thinking person whose perspective matters.

Explore both sides of their ambivalence (remember section 3.4): "What do you enjoy about drinking at parties?" "What concerns do you have about it, if any?" "What would be the benefits of drinking less or not at all?" "What would be hard about that?"

Most teens have mixed feelings. Part of them likes the social aspect, the buzz, the rebellion. Part of them worries about consequences, health, getting caught. Explore both sides without pushing.

Develop discrepancy using their own values (section 7.1): "You mentioned wanting to run track this spring. How does vaping fit with that?" "You've talked about trust being important to you. How does lying about where you're going affect that?"

Connect their substance use to things they care about. Not to shame them, but to help them see the conflict for themselves.

Provide factual information when appropriate, but only after listening: "Can I share something I learned about THC and the teenage brain?"

Not: "Let me tell you all the ways this is destroying your brain!"

10.4 The Vape Discovery Dialogue

Let's look at a complete conversation using MI when you discover substance use.

Background: Maria finds a vape pen in her daughter Elena's backpack. Elena is 15. Maria's first instinct is panic and anger. Instead, she takes a breath and uses MI.

Maria: "Elena, I found something in your backpack. A vape pen. I want to talk about it, but I want to really hear from you first. Can we talk?" (Direct but not accusatory opening)

Elena: (panicked) "I was just holding it for a friend!"

Maria: "Okay. Tell me more about that." (Not immediately calling it a lie, genuinely listening)

Elena: (realizing Mom isn't freaking out) "Actually, that's not true. It's mine."

Maria: "I appreciate your honesty. How long have you been vaping?" (Affirming truth-telling)

Elena: "A few months."

Maria: "And what made you start?" (Open question, genuinely curious)

Elena: "I don't know. My friends do it. It seemed fun."

Maria: "So your friends vape and you wanted to be part of that." (Reflection)

Elena: "Yeah."

Maria: "What do you like about it?" (Understanding the appeal)

Elena: "It's relaxing. And it tastes good. And honestly, it feels kind of cool."

Maria: "It helps you relax, you enjoy the flavor, and there's a social aspect to it." (Reflection without judgment)

Elena: "Yeah."

Maria: "What concerns do you have about it, if any?" (Exploring the other side)

Elena: "I mean, I know it's not healthy. And I'd be in huge trouble if you guys found out." (Pause) "Which I guess you did."

Maria: "So you're aware of health risks and the fact that we wouldn't approve." (Reflection)

Elena: "Yeah."

Maria: "Do the health risks worry you at all?" (Following up)

Elena: "A little. I read that it can affect your lungs. And I don't want to get actually addicted."

Maria: "You're concerned about lung damage and addiction." (Reflection of change talk)

Elena: "Yeah. Some of my friends are like, really addicted. They can't go two hours without hitting their vape."

Maria: "That worries you, seeing them that dependent on it." (Reflection)

Elena: "Kind of, yeah."

Maria: "Can I share what I know about vaping and then hear what you think?" (Asking permission)

Elena: "Okay."

94

Maria: "Vaping nicotine is highly addictive, especially for teenage brains that are still developing. Most people who start think they won't get addicted, but nicotine changes your brain chemistry pretty quickly. The other thing is we don't know the long-term lung effects yet because vaping is so new. I know you love soccer. Lung capacity matters for that." (Brief, factual information tied to her values)

Elena: "Yeah, I've noticed I get winded faster than I used to."

Maria: "You're connecting it to decreased performance." (Reflection)

Elena: "Maybe."

Maria: "What are you thinking about all this?" (Open question)

Elena: "I don't know. I don't want to be addicted. And I don't want it to mess up soccer. But I also don't want to be the only one not vaping."

Maria: "So you're weighing the costs against the social piece." (Reflection of ambivalence)

Elena: "Yeah."

Maria: "That's a real dilemma. What feels most important to you?" (Helping her prioritize)

Elena: (thinking) "Honestly, soccer matters more than fitting in with the vaping crowd."

Maria: "If you decided to stop, what would make that easier?" (Evocative question)

Elena: "I don't know. Maybe if I just said I quit. My real friends wouldn't care."

Maria: "You think your true friends would support that choice." (Reflection)

Elena: "Yeah."

Maria: "What can I do to support you?" (Offering help, not imposing it)

Elena: "Just... don't freak out if I mess up? Like, if I vape again, I don't want to be grounded forever."

Maria: "I appreciate you being honest with me. Here's what I'm thinking. I can't say there are no consequences. But I care more about you being honest and safe than about punishing you. If you're trying to quit and you slip up, I want you to be able to tell me. Does that seem fair?" (Balancing accountability with support)

Elena: "Yeah, that seems okay."

Notice what Maria accomplished. She learned the truth. Elena admitted to vaping and expressed genuine concern about it. Elena talked herself into quitting based on her own values. And their relationship stayed intact, making future conversations possible.

10.5 Rebuilding Trust

When teens have been hiding substance use, trust is broken. They've lied about where they were, what they were doing, who they were with. You feel betrayed. They feel caught.

Rebuilding trust is a process, not an event. It happens through consistent follow-through on both sides.

For parents, rebuilding trust means:

- Not constantly bringing up past mistakes
- Acknowledging efforts to change
- Slowly loosening restrictions as they demonstrate responsibility
- Separating the behavior from the person

"I'm disappointed in the choice you made, but I love you and believe you can make better choices."

For teens, rebuilding trust means:

- Being honest, even when it's hard
- Following through on agreements
- Accepting that trust is earned back gradually
- Understanding that consequences are about the behavior, not about them as a person

Use MI to collaborate on what rebuilding looks like:

"Trust has been damaged. What do you think would help rebuild it?"

"What would I see that would tell me you're making different choices?"

"What support do you need from me to make those changes?"

Let your teen have input on how they earn trust back. This increases buy-in and makes them more likely to follow through.

10.6 When to Get Help

Sometimes substance use is beyond what you can handle with conversations alone. Professional help is needed when:

- Use is frequent and interfering with daily functioning
- Your teen can't stop despite wanting to
- They're using to cope with mental health issues
- Use has led to dangerous situations
- They're using alone or using harder drugs
- Family intervention hasn't made a difference

Getting help doesn't mean you've failed. It means you're taking the problem seriously.

Frame professional help collaboratively:

"I'm worried that substance use has become a bigger problem than we can handle on our own. What do you think about talking to someone who specializes in helping teens with this?"

Not: "You're addicted. We're sending you to rehab."

Even when you need to insist on professional help, you can involve your teen in the process. Let them have some choice about the therapist, the program, the approach. People are more likely to engage with treatment they had a say in choosing.

10.7 What This Means

Substance use is terrifying for parents. But fear-driven responses push teens away exactly when they need connection most.

Using MI means you stay calm, stay curious, and stay connected. You explore their thinking, help them recognize their own concerns, and support their own motivation to make safer choices.

You can be clear about your values and expectations while also being realistic about the world your teen lives in. You can hope for abstinence while also preparing them to make safer choices if they do experiment.

Most importantly, you can maintain a relationship where your teen feels safe coming to you, even about choices you wish they weren't making. That ongoing connection is what keeps them safest.

The next chapter extends these MI principles to other risky behaviors like sex, driving, and peer pressure.

Chapter 11.0: Risky Behaviors and Independence

Your 16-year-old wants to go to an unsupervised party. Your 17-year-old has started dating someone you've never met. Your teen says they'll be "out with friends" but won't specify where. Every request feels like a test: do you trust them or tighten control?

This is the tightrope of parenting teenagers. They need to practice independence while their brains are still developing judgment. You need to keep them safe while letting them grow up. There's no perfect answer. But MI gives you tools to navigate this tension.

This chapter shows you how to have conversations about sex, driving, parties, and peer pressure that honor both safety and autonomy.

11.1 Safety Without Control

Traditional parenting approaches to risky behavior often swing between two extremes: control or permissiveness.

Control says: "No parties. No dating until you're 18. I track your location at all times. If I don't trust the situation, you don't go."

Permissiveness says: "You're almost an adult. Make your own choices. I'm here if you need me."

Neither extreme works well. Over-control prevents teens from developing judgment. They either rebel or remain dependent. Permissiveness puts teens in situations they're not ready to navigate.

MI offers a third way: **collaborative safety**. You acknowledge your teen needs increasing freedom while also being honest about your concerns. You work together to find solutions that address both.

"I understand you want to go to this party. I'm concerned because there won't be adults there and I know there will be drinking. Let's talk about how we can make this work in a way that respects your independence and addresses my safety concerns."

This isn't a trick to get them to agree with your restrictions. It's genuine collaboration. You're taking both perspectives seriously.

Marcus used this approach when his son Terrell, 17, wanted to drive to a concert two hours away with friends. Marcus's first instinct was "absolutely not." But he caught himself and used MI instead.

Marcus: "Tell me about this concert. What appeals to you about going?"

Terrell: "It's my favorite band. All my friends are going. It would be an amazing night."

Marcus: "So it's about the music and being with your friends." (Reflection)

Terrell: "Yeah."

Marcus: "I hear that. Can I share my concerns?" (Asking permission)

Terrell: "Sure."

Marcus: "Two hours on the highway, late at night, with new drivers. That worries me. Not because I don't trust you, but because of all the variables. Other drivers, fatigue on the way home, the road conditions."

Terrell: "I'm a good driver. And we'd be careful."

Marcus: "I believe you're a good driver. And at the same time, experience matters. You've had your license for six months." (Affirming while maintaining the concern)

Terrell: "So you're saying I can't go?"

Marcus: "I'm saying let's figure out if there's a way to make it work that addresses the safety piece. What if an experienced driver went with you? Or what if you took the train instead of driving?" (Collaborative problem-solving)

Terrell: "Jamie's older brother is going. He's been driving for three years."

Marcus: "Okay, so an experienced driver would be there. That helps. What about the late drive home?"

Terrell: "We could stay at Jamie's brother's apartment and drive back the next morning."

Marcus: "So you're thinking: experienced driver in the car, stay overnight instead of driving home late." (Summary)

Terrell: "Yeah. Would that work?"

Marcus: "That addresses my main concerns. Let me think about it and talk to Jamie's parents to confirm the plan. If this all checks out, I think we can make it work."

Notice what happened. Marcus didn't just say yes or no. He explored the request, shared his concerns honestly, and problem-solved collaboratively. Terrell felt heard and respected. Marcus got reasonable safety measures. Their relationship strengthened through the process.

11.2 The Both And Approach

Parenting teens requires holding two truths at once: they need increasing freedom AND they're not fully mature yet. They deserve trust AND they need limits. This is the **both/and approach**.

"I trust you AND I'm not comfortable with you being completely unsupervised at this party."

"You're mature for your age AND your brain is still developing judgment about risk."

"You deserve privacy AND I need to know where you are for safety reasons."

Both/and thinking avoids the all-or-nothing trap. You don't have to choose between complete trust and total restriction. You can honor both your teen's growing capabilities and your ongoing responsibility for their wellbeing.

This shows up in how you talk about risky situations:

Not: "I trust you completely, so do whatever you want." Not: "I don't trust you at all, so you're not going anywhere." But: "I trust your judgment in a lot of areas. And in situations with alcohol or peer pressure, even trustworthy people make impulsive choices. Let's talk about how to set you up for success."

The both/and approach acknowledges complexity. It resists binary thinking. And it models for your teen how to hold multiple perspectives at once.

11.3 Dating and Sexuality Talks

Many parents avoid conversations about sex because they're uncomfortable, don't know what to say, or worry that talking about it encourages it.

But teens are thinking about sex and dating regardless of whether you talk about them. The question isn't whether they'll have these experiences. It's whether they'll navigate them with or without your input.

Using MI for sex and dating conversations means:

Starting with their perspective: "What are you thinking about dating at this point in your life?" "What have you learned about sex and relationships from friends or school?" "What questions do you have?"

Sharing your values without imposing them: "In our family, we believe sex is something for committed relationships." "I want you to wait until you're older because I think emotional readiness matters as much as physical readiness."

Then follow with: "What do you think about that?"

You can state your values clearly while also leaving space for their perspective. This is very different from "You better not have sex or you're grounded until you're 30."

Focusing on safety and respect: Even if you hope your teen waits, prepare them for reality. Discuss consent, contraception, STIs, emotional readiness, and healthy relationships.

"I hope you'll wait. And if you don't, I want you to know how to protect yourself and make sure any relationship is respectful and consensual."

Making yourself available: "This might feel awkward to talk about. It feels awkward for me too. But I want you to know you can come to me with questions or concerns, even about uncomfortable topics."

Here's how Isabella approached a dating conversation with her daughter Sofia, 16, who'd started seeing someone.

Isabella: "You and Marcus have been spending a lot of time together. How's that going?" (Open question)

Sofia: "It's good. I really like him."

Isabella: "What do you like about him?" (Getting curious)

Sofia: "He's funny. And he actually listens when I talk, you know? Not like some guys who just talk about themselves."

Isabella: "So he's good company and makes you feel heard." (Reflection)

Sofia: "Yeah."

Isabella: "Can I ask you something? What does being in a relationship mean to you at this point?" (Exploring her thinking)

Sofia: "I don't know. Spending time together. Texting. Maybe eventually more, I guess."

Isabella: "When you say eventually more, what are you thinking?" (Following up gently)

Sofia: (uncomfortable) "I don't know. We haven't really talked about it."

Isabella: "Okay. I know this is awkward to talk about with your mom. But I want to make sure you're thinking about stuff like boundaries and safety." (Acknowledging discomfort, stating intention)

Sofia: "We're not having sex, if that's what you're asking."

Isabella: "I appreciate you telling me that. What I'm saying is, if things do progress at some point, I want you to feel prepared. To know about consent and protection and making sure any physical relationship is something you both really want." (Providing information without assuming)

Sofia: "Okay."

Isabella: "What's your understanding of consent?" (Checking knowledge)

Sofia: "It means both people want to do something and they're clear about it."

Isabella: "That's exactly right. Consent is ongoing. Just because you said yes to one thing doesn't mean you've said yes to everything. You can always change your mind." (Reinforcing and expanding)

Sofia: "I know, Mom."

Isabella: "I know you know. I'm just making sure we're on the same page. The other thing I want you to know is, if you ever feel pressured or uncomfortable, even with someone you care about, that's not okay. And you can always talk to me." (Setting clear expectation while offering support)

Sofia: "Okay. Thanks, I guess."

Isabella: "One more thing. If you do become sexually active at some point, I'd rather you talk to me about protection than hide it and be unsafe. I'm not saying I'm giving you permission. I'm saying I care more about your health than enforcing rules." (Harm reduction framing)

This conversation wasn't comfortable for either of them. But Isabella opened a door that will make future conversations easier. Sofia knows she can come to her mom, even about topics that feel awkward.

11.4 Peer Pressure Without Preaching

"If your friends jumped off a bridge, would you?" This classic line has probably never convinced a single teenager to resist peer pressure.

Teens know, logically, that they shouldn't do something just because everyone else is doing it. But in the moment, peer pressure is incredibly powerful. Especially for teenagers whose social brains are hyperactive (remember section 1.1).

Lecturing about peer pressure doesn't help because it dismisses the very real social needs your teen is navigating. Instead, use MI to help them think through how they want to handle pressure situations.

Explore their experience with peer pressure: "Have you ever felt pressured to do something you weren't sure about? What was that like?" "How do you usually handle it when friends want you to do something you're not comfortable with?"

Acknowledge the social reality: "It's really hard to be the only one not doing something. The social cost is real."

Help them problem-solve strategies: "If you're at a party and people are drinking, what are some ways you could handle it?" "What would you say if someone pressured you to get in a car with a driver who'd been drinking?"

Role-play if they're open to it: "Want to practice? I'll be the friend pressuring you, and you try out different responses."

This might feel silly, but practicing responses builds confidence. Your teen is more likely to use a strategy they've rehearsed.

Focus on their values and identity: "What kind of person do you want to be? How do you want to make decisions?"

When teens have a clear sense of their values, peer pressure has less power. "I don't drink" is easier to stick with than trying to decide in the moment at every party.

11.5 The Party Scenario

Let's see a complete MI conversation about parties and alcohol.

Background: Aisha's daughter Layla, 16, asks to go to a party. Aisha knows there will be alcohol. This is not hypothetical.

Aisha: "Tell me about this party. What's the plan?" (Information gathering)

Layla: "It's at Jordan's house. His parents are away. Just people from school hanging out."

Aisha: "How many people?" (Getting specifics)

Layla: "Maybe 20 or 30?"

Aisha: "And what do you know about what will be there? Will there be drinking?" (Direct question about alcohol)

Layla: "Probably. I mean, yeah."

Aisha: "Okay. I appreciate your honesty. What's your plan around that?" (Not freaking out, genuinely asking)

Layla: "I wasn't planning to drink."

Aisha: "Okay. And if that changes, or if you're in a situation where you're not comfortable, what then?" (Exploring her contingency plan)

Layla: "I'd text you or get a ride with someone sober."

Aisha: "Let's talk about that. Here's what I want: if you or your friends have been drinking, or if the situation feels unsafe for any reason, I want you to call me. I'll come get you, no questions asked that night, no punishment. Your safety matters more than rules." (Harm reduction offer)

Layla: "Really?"

Aisha: "Really. I'd rather you call me than make an unsafe choice because you're scared of getting in trouble." (Reinforcing)

Layla: "Okay."

Aisha: "Now, let me be clear. I'm not giving you permission to drink. I'm saying if it happens, prioritize safety. Can we talk about why I'd prefer you didn't drink?" (Asking permission to share perspective)

Layla: "Sure."

Aisha: "Alcohol affects judgment. Even people who think they're being careful make impulsive choices when they're drinking. And at your age, your brain is still developing. Regular alcohol use can actually affect how your brain develops." (Brief factual information)

Layla: "I'm not going to drink every weekend. It's just this one party."

Aisha: "I hear that. And here's the thing: one party can have consequences if something goes wrong. Sexual assault, accidents, arrests. I'm not trying to scare you. I'm being real about risk." (Honest about consequences without catastrophizing)

Layla: "I'll be careful."

Aisha: "I believe you'll try to be. And judgment gets impaired. So let's make a clear plan. You won't drink. You'll text me when you get there and when you're leaving. You'll call if anything feels off. And we have a code word: if you text me 'headache,' I'll call you immediately and pretend there's a family emergency so you have an excuse to leave. Sound good?" (Collaborative safety plan)

Layla: "Yeah. That works."

Aisha: "What time should I expect you home?"

Layla: "Midnight?"

Aisha: "How about 11:30?"

Layla: "Okay, 11:30."

Aisha: "And Layla? Thank you for being honest with me about the alcohol. That makes it easier for me to trust you." (Affirming the honesty)

This conversation sets up safety without trying to impose unrealistic control. Layla knows her mom's expectations, has a plan for managing risk, and knows she can call for help. That's as good as it gets.

11.6 Putting It Together

Risky behaviors are part of adolescence. Your teen will test limits, take chances, and make choices you wish they wouldn't. Your job isn't to prevent all risk. It's to help them develop good judgment while keeping them as safe as possible.

Using MI means you collaborate on safety, acknowledge both their need for independence and your responsibility, and stay connected even when discussing uncomfortable topics.

You share your values and concerns clearly. You also listen to their perspective and involve them in solutions. You prepare them for reality while hoping for the best.

The result isn't perfect safety. It's a relationship where your teen keeps talking to you, even about the hard stuff. And that ongoing connection is what protects them most.

The next chapter brings MI to the daily grind of chores, curfews, and household cooperation.

Chapter 12.0: Daily Cooperation and Responsibilities

"Can you please take out the trash?" Silence. Five minutes later: "I said take out the trash!" Still nothing. Ten minutes later: "Why do I have to ask you a hundred times to do ONE simple thing?!"

This scene plays out in millions of homes daily. Not over big issues like substance use or failing grades. Over mundane stuff: chores, morning routines, messy rooms, curfews. The little things that drain everyone's patience.

This chapter shows you how to apply MI to everyday cooperation, building intrinsic motivation for responsibility instead of relying on nagging and consequences.

12.1 Why Rules Feel Different

Here's something interesting. Your teen will follow some rules without question. They show up to practice on time. They meet deadlines for things they care about. They remember to charge their phone every single night.

But household rules? Those require constant reminders, battles, and consequences. Why?

Because household rules often lack the three elements that create intrinsic motivation: **autonomy**, **competence**, and **relatedness** (Deci & Ryan, 2000). Let's break this down.

Autonomy: Household rules usually feel imposed. You decided the chores, the curfew, the morning routine. Your teen had no input. Even if the rules are reasonable, they trigger resistance because they weren't chosen.

Competence: Nagging implies your teen can't remember or manage tasks on their own. This undermines their sense of capability. Why should they try when you're going to remind them anyway?

Relatedness: Rules enforced through power (because I said so) damage connection. Cooperation that comes from relationship feels different than compliance that comes from control.

When you shift from imposed rules to collaborative agreements, you tap into these three motivators. Your teen has input (autonomy), takes responsibility for remembering (competence), and cooperates because they value the relationship (relatedness).

Here's what this looked like for the Chen family. Their son Wei, 14, had morning responsibilities: wake up on time, eat breakfast, be ready for school by 7:30. Every morning was a battle. Mom nagged. Wei resisted. Everyone started the day stressed.

Mom realized the problem wasn't Wei's capability. It was the imposed system. She tried a different approach.

Mom: "Wei, our mornings are not working for either of us. I'm tired of nagging, and I'm guessing you're tired of being nagged. Want to figure out a better system together?"

Wei: (surprised) "Sure, I guess."

Mom: "What makes mornings hard for you?"

Wei: "I'm just not a morning person. I hate being rushed."

Mom: "So the time pressure and having to move fast is the worst part."

Wei: "Yeah."

Mom: "What would help?"

Wei: "I don't know. Maybe if I woke up earlier so I had more time?"

Mom: "That's interesting. You'd rather wake up earlier and have a more relaxed morning?"

Wei: "Yeah. But I can't wake up on my own. I sleep through my alarm."

Mom: "Okay, so you need a reliable wake-up method. What are some options?"

Wei: "Could you wake me up once, and then it's on me? Like, you knock on my door at 6:45, but then you don't say anything else?"

Mom: "I can do that. So I knock at 6:45, then you're responsible for getting up and getting ready. What happens if you're not ready by 7:30?"

Wei: "I don't know. Natural consequences? Like I'm late and have to deal with that?"

Mom: "I'm okay with that. Let's try it for a week. I knock once at 6:45, then you manage the rest. Sound good?"

Wei: "Yeah."

Mornings improved dramatically. Not because the rules changed, but because Wei had input and took ownership. When he did oversleep once, Mom didn't rescue him. He was late, got a tardy, and made sure it didn't happen again.

12.2 Natural Consequences Work Better

There's a difference between **punishments** and **natural consequences**.

Punishments are imposed: "You didn't do your chores, so you're grounded."

Natural consequences occur automatically: "You didn't do laundry, so you don't have clean clothes for your trip."

Punishments create resentment and don't build intrinsic motivation. Your teen complies to avoid punishment, not because they value responsibility. The lesson is "don't get caught" rather than "follow through on commitments."

Natural consequences teach actual life lessons. When you don't do laundry, you run out of clean clothes. When you don't leave on time, you're late. When you don't put gas in the car, it runs out. These consequences connect directly to the behavior in a way punishments don't.

The MI approach to household cooperation relies on natural consequences wherever possible, and when you need to add consequences, you make them logical and collaborative.

Natural consequence approach: "If you don't take your lunch, you'll be hungry at school. I'm not bringing it to you."

"If you don't put your dishes in the dishwasher, they won't get clean for next time you want to use them."

"If you miss curfew without calling, I'll worry. That makes it harder for me to trust you with flexibility next time."

Collaborative consequence approach (when natural consequences aren't sufficient): "We agreed you'd keep your room reasonably clean. If it's not done by Sunday, how should we handle it? What consequence makes sense to you?"

Let your teen help determine consequences. When they have input, they're more likely to see them as fair.

Here's how this worked for Diego and his son Miguel, 15. Miguel was supposed to mow the lawn weekly. He consistently put it off until Diego nagged him into doing it.

Diego: "Miguel, we need to talk about the lawn situation. I'm tired of reminding you. What's going on?"

Miguel: "I just forget."

Diego: "Okay. How could you remember without me having to remind you?"

Miguel: "I could set a reminder on my phone?"

Diego: "That might work. And if the reminder doesn't work and the lawn still doesn't get mowed, then what?"

Miguel: "I don't know. What do you think should happen?"

Diego: "I'm asking you. What would be a fair consequence if you agreed to do it and then didn't follow through?"

Miguel: (thinking) "Maybe I lose my allowance for that week?"

Diego: "That seems reasonable. So the plan is: you set a phone reminder, you mow by Saturday. If it's not done by Saturday evening, no allowance that week. That feel fair to you?"

Miguel: "Yeah."

By involving Miguel in setting the consequence, Diego increased buy-in. Miguel was more motivated to follow through because he'd helped create the system.

12.3 Morning and Bedtime Battles

Morning and bedtime routines are common battlegrounds because they happen every single day. The repetition wears everyone down.

Using MI for these routines means:

Understanding what makes it hard: "What's the hardest part of getting up in the morning for you?" "What gets in the way of going to bed on time?"

Often there's a specific obstacle. They can't fall asleep because they're on their phone. They hit snooze because they're exhausted. They procrastinate bedtime because it's the only alone time they get.

Problem-solving collaboratively: "What would make mornings easier?" "If you designed your ideal bedtime routine, what would it include?"

Let them generate solutions. They know what might work for them better than you do.

Setting up for success: Maybe they need everything laid out the night before. Maybe they need a loud alarm across the room. Maybe they need earlier dinners so they're not hungry at bedtime. Identify what helps and implement it together.

Jennifer's daughter Kayla, 16, was constantly exhausted because she stayed up until 1 or 2 a.m. Jennifer used to demand lights out at 10. Kayla would agree, then ignore it. Jennifer would check at 11 and find Kayla still on her phone. Every night, same battle.

Jennifer tried MI instead.

Jennifer: "Kayla, you seem exhausted all the time. What do you think is going on?"

Kayla: "I don't get enough sleep."

Jennifer: "What's keeping you up?" (Open question, not accusatory)

Kayla: "I can't fall asleep. I try, but my brain won't shut off. So I scroll on my phone until I'm tired."

Jennifer: "The scrolling helps you wind down." (Reflection)

Kayla: "Kind of. But then I'm up until 2 and I feel terrible in the morning."

Jennifer: "So it's not actually working that well." (Gentle challenge)

Kayla: "No."

Jennifer: "What do you think would help you fall asleep without the phone?" (Evocative question)

Kayla: "I don't know. Maybe if I did something relaxing before bed? Like reading?"

Jennifer: "That could work. What else?"

Kayla: "I've heard that you're not supposed to use screens right before bed because they keep you awake."

Jennifer: "That's true. The blue light affects melatonin. What time would you need to stop screens to fall asleep at a reasonable hour?" (Building on her knowledge)

Kayla: "Maybe 10:30? Then read until I'm tired?"

Jennifer: "What would help you actually stop at 10:30 instead of scrolling until 2?"

Kayla: "I could put my phone in the kitchen."

Jennifer: "Would you actually do that, or is that one of those things that sounds good but won't happen?" (Checking commitment)

Kayla: "I'd do it. I'm serious about getting more sleep. I feel like crap all the time."

Jennifer: "Okay. Let's try it. Phone in the kitchen by 10:30, read in bed until you're sleepy. We'll see how it goes for a week."

By exploring Kayla's actual experience and helping her problem-solve, Jennifer avoided the nightly battle. Kayla came up with her own solution, so she was motivated to follow through.

12.4 The Fair Curfew Negotiation

Curfew is often a major conflict point. You want your teen home at a time that feels safe. They want to stay out later with their friends. How do you find middle ground?

Using the collaborative approach we discussed in section 6.5, here's a framework for curfew negotiation:

Start with open questions: "What time feels reasonable to you for a weekend curfew?" "What are your friends' curfews?" "What would you be doing if you stayed out later?"

Share your concerns: "I worry about safety late at night. Not because I don't trust you, but because more risky things happen after midnight." "I need to be able to sleep without worrying. When you're not home, I can't relax."

Explore middle ground: "What time addresses both your desire to stay out and my need to know you're safe?" "What if we had different curfews for different situations?"

Build in flexibility with communication: "What if your base curfew is 11, but you can text and ask for extensions when there's a good reason?" "How about we try 11:30 for a month and revisit if it's working well?"

Create clear agreements: "So we're agreeing: 11 p.m. on regular weekends, midnight for special events if you ask ahead, and you text if plans change. If you're consistently on time, we'll talk about adjusting. If you're consistently late, we'll revisit. Fair?"

Here's what this looked like for Aisha and her daughter Layla, 15.

Aisha: "Your curfew right now is 10 on weekends. You've been asking for later. Let's talk about it." (Opening the conversation)

Layla: "Everyone else gets to stay out until midnight at least."

Aisha: "Your friends have later curfews." (Reflection, not arguing)

Layla: "Yeah. It's embarrassing leaving early."

Aisha: "The social cost feels high." (Understanding her concern)

Layla: "Really high."

Aisha: "Okay. I hear that. Can I share my thinking?" (Asking permission)

Layla: "Sure."

Aisha: "I worry about you being out late. Not because I don't trust you, but because I know risky stuff happens late at night. And honestly, I can't sleep well when you're not home." (Honest about concerns)

Layla: "But I'm always fine. Nothing bad happens."

Aisha: "You're right. You've been responsible. I appreciate that. So let's think about this together. What time would feel fair to you?" (Affirming, then problem-solving)

Layla: "Midnight on weekends."

Aisha: "Okay. And I'm thinking 11. Where's the middle ground?" (Negotiating)

Layla: "11:30?"

Aisha: "I could do 11:30. With a couple conditions. You text when you get where you're going and when you're heading home. And if something changes, you let me know right away. Can you do that?" (Setting expectations)

Layla: "Yeah, I can do that."

Aisha: "And if you're consistently late or I can't reach you, we revisit. But if this goes well, we can talk about adjusting as you get older." (Consequences for breaking agreement, but also room to grow)

Layla: "Okay. That seems fair."

Notice this wasn't Aisha caving or Layla getting everything she wanted. It was genuine negotiation that addressed both perspectives.

12.5 When They Don't Follow Through

Your teen agrees to the collaborative plan. Then they don't do it. Now what?

First, get curious about why. Don't immediately jump to consequences.

"We agreed you'd take out the trash on Wednesdays. It's Friday and it's still sitting there. What happened?"

Maybe they genuinely forgot. Maybe the plan wasn't realistic. Maybe they're overwhelmed with other stuff. Maybe they're testing to see if you'll enforce it.

Understanding the "why" helps you address the actual problem.

If they forgot, problem-solve memory strategies: "What would help you remember without me having to nag?"

If the plan wasn't realistic, adjust it: "Maybe Wednesdays don't work with your schedule. What day would be better?"

If they're overwhelmed, help prioritize: "You have a lot on your plate. What's most important right now?"

If they're testing limits, follow through with the agreed consequence: "We agreed that if the trash wasn't out by Thursday, you'd lose your allowance for the week. That's what happens."

The key is staying calm and matter-of-fact. Consequences aren't about anger or punishment. They're about follow-through on agreements.

Marcus's daughter Camila, 14, agreed to keep her bathroom clean. Two weeks later, it was a disaster. Marcus was frustrated but used MI.

Marcus: "Camila, we agreed you'd keep your bathroom clean. It's pretty rough in there. What's up?"

Camila: "I've been busy."

Marcus: "Too busy to spend five minutes a day on it?" (Gentle reality check)

Camila: "I guess I just forgot."

Marcus: "Okay. How can you remember?"

Camila: "I don't know."

Marcus: "Here's the thing. We made an agreement. When you don't follow through, what should the consequence be? We talked about this being your responsibility." (Referring back to agreement)

Camila: "I'll clean it this weekend."

Marcus: "Good. And going forward, what's your plan for keeping it clean without me having to remind you?"

Camila: "I could clean it every Sunday?"

Marcus: "That could work if you actually do it. What happens if Sunday comes and it's still a mess?"

Camila: "Then... I don't know. You clean my bathroom and I pay you?"

Marcus: (laughing) "I'm not cleaning your bathroom. How about this: if it's not reasonably clean by Sunday night, you lose screen time that week until it's done."

Camila: "Okay. That's fair."

By problem-solving together and referring back to their agreement, Marcus avoided a lecture while maintaining accountability.

12.6 Building Intrinsic Motivation

The ultimate goal isn't compliance. It's intrinsic motivation. You want your teen to take out the trash because they value contributing to the household, not because they're avoiding consequences.

This happens gradually through:

Connecting responsibilities to larger values: "Taking care of our home is how we show respect for each other and our space." "Following through on commitments builds trust and shows maturity."

Acknowledging their contributions: "I noticed you've been taking the trash out without reminders. That makes a real difference." "Thank you for getting your stuff done this week. It helps the whole household run more smoothly."

Giving them increasing autonomy as they demonstrate responsibility: "You've been really consistent with your chores. I'm not going to check anymore. I trust you to handle it."

Letting them experience the satisfaction of competence: When they handle things independently, step back and let them feel capable. Your recognition matters, but so does their own sense of "I can do this."

Over time, many teens shift from "I have to do this" to "this is just what I do." Not all of them, and not about everything. But the collaborative approach makes that shift more likely than the nagging/punishment cycle.

12.7 Key Takeaways

Daily cooperation and household responsibilities don't require constant battles. When you shift from imposed rules to collaborative agreements, you tap into your teen's need for autonomy, competence, and connection.

Use natural consequences when possible. They teach life lessons better than punishments. When you need to add consequences, make them logical and involve your teen in determining them.

For persistent issues like morning routines, bedtime, and curfews, explore what makes them hard and problem-solve together. When teens help create the system, they're more motivated to follow it.

When they don't follow through, get curious before getting angry. Understand why, then address the real problem. Refer back to agreements and follow through calmly on consequences.

The goal is gradual development of intrinsic motivation. You're not just getting them to comply. You're helping them become responsible people who value contributing and following through.

The next chapter tackles one of the hardest situations: the defiant, disrespectful, or difficult teen.

Chapter 13.0: The Defiant or Difficult Teen

"I hate you!" The door slams. You stand there, heart pounding, wondering what just happened and how a simple request turned into a nuclear explosion.

Some teens are easy. They push boundaries, sure, but they generally cooperate. Then there are the teens who seem to fight everything. Every request becomes an argument. Every limit triggers defiance. You feel like you're walking on eggshells, never knowing what will set them off.

This chapter shows you how to use MI with defiant, disrespectful, or genuinely difficult teens without losing your mind or your relationship.

13.1 Understanding Oppositional Behavior

First, understand what defiance actually is. It's not your teen being deliberately awful (usually). It's a response to feeling controlled, misunderstood, or threatened.

Remember from section 1.2, teens have a powerful drive for autonomy. When that drive gets blocked repeatedly, some teens become oppositional. It's like they're allergic to being told what to do. Any hint of control triggers immediate resistance.

There's also something called **oppositional defiant disorder** (ODD), a clinical diagnosis characterized by persistent angry mood, argumentative behavior, and vindictiveness. But most defiant teens don't have ODD. They're developmentally normal teens who've gotten stuck in a pattern with their parents.

That pattern usually looks like this:

1. Parent makes request or sets limit
2. Teen resists or argues
3. Parent pushes harder (raising voice, threatening consequences)
4. Teen escalates (yelling, defiance, disrespect)
5. Parent either backs down (teaching teen that escalation works) or imposes harsh consequence (damaging relationship)
6. Repeat, with each person more entrenched in their role

This cycle feeds itself. The more you try to control, the more they resist. The more they resist, the more you crack down. Before long, you're locked in a power struggle where nobody wins.

MI breaks this cycle by changing your part of the dance. When you stop pushing, they often stop pushing back.

Here's what happened with the Rodriguez family. Their son Carlos, 15, was intensely defiant. Ask him to do anything, and he'd refuse or argue. They tried everything: consequences, taking things away, stricter rules. Nothing worked. Carlos just got more oppositional.

His mom Elena learned about MI and tried a radically different approach. Instead of demanding compliance, she got curious about his experience.

Elena: "Carlos, I notice whenever I ask you to do something, you immediately resist. Help me understand what's going on for you."

Carlos: (surprised by the question) "You're always bossing me around."

Elena: "It feels like I'm controlling you." (Reflection, not defensiveness)

Carlos: "Yeah. I can't do anything without you telling me how to do it or when to do it."

Elena: "You need more autonomy." (Naming the core issue)

Carlos: "I'm not a little kid anymore."

Elena: "You're right. You're not. And maybe I'm still treating you like one sometimes. What would be different if I gave you more space?" (Acknowledging truth, exploring)

Carlos: (pause, not expecting this) "I don't know. You'd trust me more?"

Elena: "What would that look like? Trust you more?" (Getting specific)

Carlos: "Like, you'd ask instead of telling. And you wouldn't assume I'm going to screw up."

This conversation didn't solve everything. But it started to shift their dynamic. Elena began noticing how often she gave commands instead of requests. Carlos began to see that his mom was trying to change.

13.2 Staying Calm Under Fire

When your teen is yelling, being disrespectful, or outright defying you, staying calm is incredibly hard. Your body goes into fight-or-flight. Your heart races. You want to yell back or impose immediate consequences.

But reacting from that state escalates everything. Your teen's already dysregulated. If you dysregulate too, you're just two people yelling, not a parent helping a teen learn emotional regulation.

Staying calm doesn't mean you're okay with disrespect. It means you're modeling the behavior you want to see.

Strategies for staying calm:

Breathe. Literally. Take slow breaths. This activates your parasympathetic nervous system and helps you think instead of just react.

Pause before responding. You don't have to answer immediately. "I need a minute to think about this" is a completely valid response.

Lower your voice. When someone yells and you respond quietly, it often de-escalates. They have to quiet down to hear you.

Name your feelings. "I'm getting really frustrated right now. I need to step away for a few minutes before we continue this conversation."

Remember the goal. Your goal isn't to win the argument. It's to maintain the relationship while setting appropriate limits. Keep that in mind.

Have perspective. This moment feels huge. In the context of your teen's whole life, it's one interaction. Don't catastrophize.

Diego learned these strategies when his daughter Camila, 14, would explode over seemingly nothing. She'd scream, say horrible things, slam doors. Diego used to yell back. It never helped.

One day when Camila started screaming about something minor, Diego took a breath and tried something different.

Diego: (calmly) "Camila, I can see you're really upset. I want to understand what's going on, but I can't have this conversation when you're yelling at me. I'm going to step away for a few minutes. When you're ready to talk more calmly, come find me."

Then he left. Not angrily. Just removed himself from the situation.

Camila was shocked. She was used to him engaging in the fight. After 10 minutes, she came out of her room.

Camila: "I'm sorry I yelled."

Diego: "I appreciate that. What was that about?"

Camila: "I don't know. I'm just stressed about everything."

Diego: "Tell me about the stress." (Open question, genuinely listening)

By not engaging in the fight, Diego created space for a real conversation. This didn't fix everything overnight. But it showed Camila that screaming wouldn't get the reaction she was used to.

13.3 Reflective Listening for Anger

When your teen is angry, your instinct is to defend, explain, or shut it down. "Don't talk to me like that!" "You're being ridiculous!" "Go to your room until you can be respectful!"

These responses escalate anger. They don't validate the feeling, so your teen feels even more unheard and misunderstood.

Reflective listening (remember section 4.3) is powerful for angry teens because it shows you're hearing them without agreeing or condoning disrespect.

Teen: "This is so stupid! You never let me do anything!"

Shutting down: "Watch your tone. And that's not true."

Reflective listening: "You're really frustrated that I'm saying no."

Teen: "I hate living here! You're ruining my life!"

Shutting down: "You're being dramatic. Go to your room."

Reflective listening: "You're really angry right now. It feels like I'm making your life worse."

Notice what reflection does. It acknowledges the emotion without agreeing with the content. You're not saying "yes, I am ruining your life." You're saying "you feel like I'm ruining your life."

This distinction matters. It validates their experience while maintaining your perspective.

After reflecting, you can address the behavior:

"I hear that you're frustrated. And I need you to talk to me respectfully. Take a few minutes to calm down, then we can discuss this."

Here's how Jennifer used reflective listening when her son David, 16, exploded about his curfew.

David: "This curfew is ridiculous! I'm 16! You treat me like a child!"

Jennifer: "You feel like 10 p.m. is too early and infantilizing." (Reflection)

David: "Yes! Everyone else gets to stay out later!"

Jennifer: "It feels unfair compared to your friends." (Reflection)

David: "It is unfair!"

Jennifer: "You want the same freedom they have." (Reflection)

David: (starting to calm down) "Yeah."

Jennifer: "Okay. I hear that. Can we talk about this when we're both calmer? I'm willing to discuss the curfew, but I need the conversation to be respectful." (Setting limit while remaining open)

David: "Fine."

By reflecting first, Jennifer defused the immediate anger. David felt heard. Then she could set a boundary about respectful communication without it escalating further.

13.4 Setting Limits Calmly

Just because you're using MI doesn't mean you have no limits. You can be collaborative and still have non-negotiables.

The difference is how you set those limits.

Old way: "I don't care what you think. This is my house, my rules. You'll do what I say or else."

MI way: "I understand you disagree with this rule. I've heard your perspective. And this is my decision. Here's why."

You're firm, but respectful. You acknowledge their feelings while maintaining the boundary.

Clear limit-setting: "I know you're angry. And you cannot speak to me that way. When you're ready to talk respectfully, we can continue."

"I understand this feels unfair. The answer is still no."

"I've heard your concerns. I'm making a different choice. I know that's disappointing."

The key is staying calm, acknowledging their feelings, and holding the line without getting drawn into a fight.

Some limits are about safety and aren't negotiable: "You cannot drive after drinking. That's a hard line." "You will not skip school. That's not up for debate."

Other limits have more room for discussion: "Let's talk about curfew and see if we can find something that works for both of us." "I'm open to revisiting the phone rules if you can show me you can manage screen time."

Know which category your limits fall into, and be clear with your teen.

Marcus learned this with his son Terrell, 17, who wanted to quit his part-time job to have more free time.

Terrell: "I'm quitting my job. I hate it and I need more time for myself."

Marcus: "You're burned out and need a break." (Reflection)

Terrell: "Yeah."

Marcus: "I get that. And here's my perspective. You committed to this job through the summer. You need to honor that commitment. Quitting partway through teaches the wrong lesson." (Firm limit with reasoning)

Terrell: "That's not fair! You can't make me keep working!"

Marcus: "You're right. I can't make you. But if you quit without notice before the summer is over, I won't help you pay for car insurance anymore. You want the freedom that comes with having a car, you need to demonstrate the responsibility that goes with it." (Natural consequence)

Terrell: "That's blackmail!"

Marcus: "I can see why it feels that way. I'm connecting your choices to consequences. You have autonomy here. You can quit the job. And I have autonomy to decide how I support you financially based on the responsibility you show." (Staying calm, maintaining limit)

Terrell was furious. But Marcus didn't back down or escalate. He held the limit calmly while acknowledging Terrell's feelings.

13.5 When Defiance Signals Deeper Issues

Sometimes persistent defiance signals something more than normal teenage boundary-testing. It can indicate:

- **Depression or anxiety**: Sometimes anger is how these present in teens
- **Trauma**: Past experiences can make teens hypervigilant to control
- **Learning disabilities**: Constant frustration at school can spill over at home
- **Substance use**: Changes in behavior can signal hidden substance issues
- **Family conflict**: Defiance toward one parent may reflect loyalty conflicts

- **Undiagnosed ADHD**: Impulsivity and emotional dysregulation can look like defiance

If your teen's behavior has changed significantly, if they're defiant across all settings (not just with you), if they're also showing signs of depression or anxiety, or if your relationship has deteriorated to the point where you can barely communicate, consider getting professional help.

A therapist can help determine if there's an underlying issue and work with your family on more effective communication patterns.

Frame professional help collaboratively:

"I've noticed our relationship has gotten really difficult. I'm wondering if it would help to talk to someone together, get some outside perspective on how we can communicate better. What do you think?"

Not: "You have serious behavioral problems. You need therapy."

Chen's daughter Mei, 15, had become increasingly defiant over several months. She'd always been strong-willed, but this was different. Angry outbursts, refusal to follow any rules, cruel comments.

Chen initially tried stricter consequences. That made it worse. Then he tried MI. That helped a little, but something still felt off.

Finally, he suggested family therapy. Mei resisted at first, but after a few sessions, it came out that she was being bullied at school and felt like she had no control over anything. The defiance at home was where she could exert some power.

Once they understood the real issue, they could address it. The defiance didn't disappear overnight, but it made sense in context. Mei needed help with the bullying situation and tools for coping with feeling powerless. The family therapy helped them rebuild their relationship.

13.6 The I Hate You Response

"I hate you!" might be the most painful thing a parent hears. It cuts deep. Your first instinct might be to punish them for saying it, or to say something hurtful back, or to collapse into guilt and fear that they really do hate you.

None of those responses help.

Here's what "I hate you" usually means:

- "I'm so angry right now and I don't know how to express it"
- "You're setting a limit I don't like and I want you to feel bad"
- "I feel powerless and this is how I fight back"
- "I'm hurting and anger is easier than vulnerability"

It almost never means "I genuinely hate you as a person and wish you weren't in my life."

How to respond:

Acknowledge the feeling without taking the bait: "I can hear how angry you are right now." "You're really upset with me."

Don't engage with the content: "I love you, even when you're angry with me." "I know you don't really hate me. You hate the situation."

Give space: "I'm going to give you some time to cool down. We can talk when you're ready."

Later, when calm, address it: "Earlier you said you hated me. I know you were really angry. That was hurtful to hear, though. Can we talk about better ways to express anger?"

Isabella's daughter Sofia, 14, screamed "I hate you!" after Isabella said no to a sleepover.

Isabella wanted to scream back or ground Sofia for being disrespectful. Instead, she took a breath.

Isabella: "I hear how angry you are that I said no." (Acknowledging feeling)

Sofia: "You're the worst parent ever!"

Isabella: "You're really upset right now. I'm going to step away and let you calm down. When you're ready to talk about this respectfully, I'm here." (Setting limit, giving space)

She left the room. An hour later, Sofia came to find her.

128

Sofia: "I'm sorry I said I hate you."

Isabella: "Thank you. That was really hurtful to hear. I know you were angry, but there are better ways to express that. Can we talk about what you were actually feeling?" (Accepting apology, teaching)

Sofia: "I just felt like you don't trust me. All my friends are going."

Isabella: "So it felt like a trust issue, not just about this specific sleepover." (Reflection getting to real issue)

Sofia: "Yeah."

By not reacting to the "I hate you," Isabella created space for the real conversation about trust.

13.7 Moving Forward

Defiant, difficult teens are exhausting. They test your patience, trigger your worst parenting impulses, and make you question everything.

But defiance is often a response to feeling controlled or misunderstood. When you stop pushing and start listening, when you offer autonomy instead of imposing limits, many defiant teens begin to soften.

This doesn't happen overnight. Patterns built over years take time to change. You'll mess up. You'll lose your temper. You'll slip back into old patterns. That's normal.

What matters is the overall direction. Are you moving toward collaboration? Are you staying calmer? Are you reflecting more and reacting less? Progress, not perfection.

And if defiance persists despite your best efforts, or if it signals deeper issues, don't hesitate to get professional support. Some situations need more help than a parenting book can provide.

The next chapter addresses perhaps the scariest topic for parents: mental health concerns.

Chapter 14.0: Mental Health and Wellbeing

You notice your teen sleeping all the time. Or not sleeping at all. Withdrawing from friends. Seeming hopeless. Making comments about not wanting to be here anymore. Terror grips you. This is beyond normal teenage moodiness. Something is really wrong.

Mental health concerns in teens are more common than most parents realize. Anxiety, depression, self-harm, eating disorders, and suicidal thoughts affect millions of teenagers. And having these conversations is one of the hardest things you'll ever do as a parent.

This chapter shows you how to use MI to open the door to difficult mental health conversations, support your struggling teen, and collaborate with professionals when needed.

14.1 Opening the Door

Many parents avoid mental health conversations because they don't know what to say or they're afraid of making it worse. So they wait, hoping the problem will resolve on its own. Meanwhile, their teen suffers alone, thinking nobody notices or cares.

The first step is simply opening the door. Letting your teen know you see their struggle and you're there for them.

Opening the conversation: "I've noticed you seem really down lately. I'm worried about you. Can we talk about what's going on?"

"You've been spending a lot of time alone in your room. I'm wondering how you're doing."

"I care about you, and I can tell something's been hard for you. I'm here to listen if you want to talk."

Keep it simple. Express concern, not judgment. Invite conversation without demanding it.

Your teen might open up immediately. More likely, they'll say "I'm fine" or "nothing's wrong." Don't force it.

"Okay. I just want you to know I'm here when you're ready to talk. I love you."

Then watch for another opportunity. Sometimes it takes multiple gentle invitations before a teen is ready to share.

Here's what happened with the Thompson family. Their son Lucas, 16, had been withdrawing for months. He used to be social and engaged. Now he barely spoke, spent all his time alone, seemed exhausted despite sleeping constantly.

His mom Rachel was terrified but didn't know how to bring it up. Finally, she tried a simple approach.

Rachel: "Lucas, can I talk to you for a minute?"

Lucas: "I guess."

Rachel: "I've noticed you seem really different lately. More withdrawn, sleeping a lot. I'm concerned about you. How are you really doing?"

Lucas: (long pause) "I don't know. Not great, I guess."

Rachel: "Tell me more about not great." (Open invitation)

Lucas: "I just... I don't feel like doing anything. Everything feels pointless."

Rachel: (resisting urge to fix or reassure) "That sounds really hard. How long have you been feeling this way?" (Staying curious)

Lucas: "I don't know. A few months?"

Rachel: "A few months. That's a long time to carry that alone." (Acknowledgment)

Lucas: (tears starting) "I didn't know how to tell you."

Rachel: "I'm glad you're telling me now. I want to help. What would help look like for you?" (Offering support, not imposing solutions)

This conversation didn't solve Lucas's depression. But it opened the door for him to get help. Rachel listened without judgment, stayed curious instead of panicking, and offered support without taking over.

14.2 When They Resist Help

Your teen is clearly struggling, but they refuse to talk about it or get help. This is terrifying and frustrating. You can see they need support, but you can't force them to accept it.

Using MI means you explore their resistance instead of arguing with it.

"I'm worried about you and I think talking to someone might help. You don't seem interested in that. Help me understand what gets in the way."

Common reasons teens resist mental health help:

- Stigma: "I'm not crazy"
- Fear: "What if they lock me up or tell my friends?"
- Hopelessness: "Nothing will help anyway"
- Shame: "I should be able to handle this myself"
- Distrust: "Therapists just want to analyze me"
- Autonomy: "You can't make me"

Once you understand their specific concern, you can address it.

"You're worried about stigma. I get that. What if we found someone who specializes in teens, someone who really gets what you're going through?"

"You're scared about what therapy means. What if we just tried a couple sessions and see how it feels? You can always stop if it's not helpful."

"It feels hopeless right now. I can't promise therapy will fix everything. But doing nothing definitely won't help. Would you be willing to try?"

Here's how Diego approached it with his daughter Camila, 15, who was showing signs of severe anxiety but refused to see a therapist.

Diego: "Camila, I'm really worried about you. The anxiety seems to be getting worse. I think it would help to talk to someone who specializes in this."

Camila: "I'm not going to a therapist. That's for crazy people."

Diego: "You think seeing a therapist means you're crazy." (Reflection of concern)

Camila: "Yeah. I'm not crazy."

Diego: "You're absolutely not crazy. You're struggling with anxiety, which is incredibly common. Millions of people get help for anxiety. It doesn't mean you're broken or crazy. It means you're dealing with something hard and getting support for it." (Reframing)

Camila: "I don't want to talk to a stranger about my problems."

Diego: "That makes sense. It does feel weird to open up to someone you don't know. What if we found someone who really gets teen anxiety? Someone who's helped other people with exactly what you're going through?" (Addressing the concern)

Camila: "I guess."

Diego: "What would make you willing to try it? What would a therapist need to be like for you to feel okay talking to them?" (Evocative question)

Camila: "I don't know. Someone who doesn't make me feel like a patient?"

Diego: "Okay. So someone who treats you like a person, not a case study. I can look for that. Would you be willing to try one session and see how it feels?" (Building on her answer)

Camila: "One session. But if I hate it, I'm not going back."

Diego: "Fair enough. One session, and then we talk about whether it's helpful."

By exploring her resistance instead of arguing with it, Diego helped Camila move from "absolutely not" to "I'll try one session." That's progress.

14.3 Supporting Without Rescuing

When your teen is struggling with mental health issues, your instinct is to fix it. Take away their pain. Solve the problem. But you can't fix depression or anxiety for them. Trying to rescue them can actually make things worse.

Rescuing looks like:

- Doing everything for them because they're struggling
- Making all their decisions to reduce stress
- Calling them in sick constantly to avoid anxiety triggers
- Removing all challenges from their life
- Becoming their therapist instead of their parent

Supporting looks like:

- Acknowledging their struggle while maintaining appropriate expectations
- Helping them problem-solve rather than solving for them
- Encouraging them to use coping skills their therapist teaches
- Balancing compassion with accountability
- Being present without taking over

The difference is this: rescuing keeps them dependent. Supporting builds their capability to manage their mental health.

Jennifer learned this with her daughter Kayla, 16, who had severe social anxiety. Jennifer's initial response was to let Kayla avoid everything that made her anxious. She could skip school events, decline social invitations, stay home when overwhelmed.

Kayla's therapist gently pointed out that avoidance was reinforcing the anxiety. Kayla needed support to gradually face anxiety-provoking situations, not permission to avoid them entirely.

Jennifer had to find a middle ground:

"I know going to the school assembly makes you really anxious. And I also know that avoiding it completely reinforces the anxiety. What would make it manageable for you? Could you go for part of it? Could you take a friend? What support would help you do this hard thing?"

This balanced empathy (acknowledging the genuine difficulty) with encouragement (helping her face the fear rather than avoid it).

Supporting mental health means:

- Validating their feelings without making feelings the whole story
- Encouraging therapy engagement and skill practice
- Maintaining routines and expectations (with appropriate flexibility)
- Checking in without hovering

- Celebrating small wins
- Knowing when to push gently and when to back off

14.4 The Depression Concern Dialogue

Let's see how an MI conversation about depression might unfold.

Background: Marcus has noticed his daughter Zoe, 15, showing signs of depression. She's withdrawn, sleeping excessively, grades dropping, lost interest in activities she used to love. He's worried and wants to help.

Marcus: "Zoe, can we talk? I've been noticing some things and I'm concerned." (Opening gently)

Zoe: "What things?"

Marcus: "You seem really down. You're sleeping a lot, you've stopped doing things you used to enjoy, and you just seem sad most of the time. I'm worried about you." (Specific observations, expressing concern)

Zoe: "I'm just tired."

Marcus: "You're exhausted. What's making you so tired?" (Reflection plus open question)

Zoe: (shrugs) "I don't know. Everything, I guess."

Marcus: "Everything feels heavy right now." (Reflection)

Zoe: (tears starting) "Yeah."

Marcus: "How long have you been feeling this way?" (Gathering information)

Zoe: "I don't know. A while. A few months maybe."

Marcus: "That's a long time to feel like this. Have you thought about talking to someone about it?" (Gently introducing idea of help)

Zoe: "Like who?"

Marcus: "Like a therapist or counselor. Someone who specializes in helping people when they're feeling depressed." (Specific suggestion)

Zoe: "I'm not depressed."

Marcus: "Okay. What would you call how you're feeling?" (Not arguing with the label, staying curious)

Zoe: "I don't know. Just... blah. Like nothing matters."

Marcus: "Nothing feels meaningful or important right now." (Reflection)

Zoe: "Yeah."

Marcus: "That sounds really hard. And it also sounds like depression, even if that word feels scary. Depression isn't something to be ashamed of. It's really common, and it's treatable." (Psychoeducation without forcing the label)

Zoe: "How would a therapist even help?"

Marcus: "That's a good question. A therapist could help you figure out what's going on, give you tools to manage these feelings, and help you feel more like yourself again. It doesn't mean you're broken. It means you're going through something hard and getting support for it." (Explaining value without overpromising)

Zoe: "I guess I could try it."

Marcus: "I think that's really brave. We'll find someone good. And if the first person doesn't feel like a good fit, we'll find someone else. The important thing is you're willing to try." (Affirming willingness, setting realistic expectations)

Notice Marcus didn't diagnose, catastrophize, or force anything. He observed, expressed concern, stayed curious, and offered support. He made space for Zoe to consider help without demanding it.

14.5 Working With Professionals

When your teen is in therapy, your role shifts. You're not the therapist. You're the parent who supports what happens in therapy.

This means:

- Letting therapy be private space (unless there's a safety concern)
- Attending family sessions when the therapist recommends

- Implementing strategies the therapist suggests
- Communicating with the therapist while respecting teen's privacy
- Being patient with the process

Some parents want constant updates on what's discussed in therapy. Resist this urge. Teens need to know therapy is confidential (within safety limits) or they won't be honest.

You can check in generally: "How did therapy go today?" "Is the therapist helpful?" "Anything you want to talk about from your session?"

But don't interrogate or demand details.

If the therapist suggests changes (different sleep schedule, limiting phone use, exposure exercises for anxiety), implement them supportively:

"Your therapist suggested we work on a better sleep routine. Let's figure out together what would help."

Not: "Your therapist said you need to go to bed earlier, so that's the new rule."

Collaborate with your teen to implement therapeutic recommendations using the MI skills from earlier chapters.

14.6 When to Seek Emergency Help

Some situations require immediate professional intervention, not MI conversations:

Seek emergency help if your teen:

- Talks about suicide or wanting to die
- Has a suicide plan
- Engages in serious self-harm
- Shows signs of psychosis (hallucinations, delusions, completely disconnected from reality)
- Has severely restricted eating to dangerous levels
- Is using substances in ways that pose immediate danger

In these situations:

- Take it seriously

- Don't leave them alone
- Call 988 (Suicide and Crisis Lifeline) or go to the emergency room
- Remove access to means of self-harm
- Get professional assessment immediately

You can still use MI principles while getting emergency help:

"I'm really worried about what you just said about not wanting to be alive. I love you and I need to make sure you're safe. We're going to talk to someone who can help right now."

Not: "You're crazy. We're going to the hospital."

Even in crisis, your tone and approach matter.

14.7 Parent Self Care

Supporting a teen with mental health struggles is exhausting and emotionally draining. You need support too.

Take care of yourself:

- Get your own therapy if needed
- Join a support group for parents
- Lean on friends, partner, extended family
- Practice stress management
- Don't make your teen's mental health your entire identity
- Remember you're doing your best in a hard situation

You can't pour from an empty cup. Taking care of yourself isn't selfish. It's necessary for being able to show up for your teen.

And remember, mental health struggles don't mean you failed as a parent. Depression, anxiety, and other mental health issues have complex causes including genetics, environment, life experiences, and brain chemistry. Your teen's mental health challenges are not your fault.

What matters is how you respond. Are you getting them help? Are you providing support? Are you learning what helps and what doesn't?

You're reading this book, which means you're trying. That matters.

14.8 The Bottom Line

Mental health conversations are scary. But they're also necessary. Your teen needs to know you see their struggle and you're there for them.

Use MI to open the door, explore their perspective, and collaborate on getting help. Support without rescuing. Work with professionals while respecting therapy boundaries. And take care of yourself in the process.

Mental health challenges are tough, but they're also treatable. With support, therapy, and sometimes medication, most teens improve significantly. Your ongoing connection and support throughout that process makes a real difference.

You've now worked through the entire MI toolkit and seen how to apply it to every major challenge parents face with teens. The remaining chapters help you put it all together and build the skills for long-term success.

Chapter 15.0: From Conversation to Action

You've had great MI conversations. Your teen has talked about wanting to change. They've recognized the gap between their behavior and their values. They've expressed commitment. And then... nothing changes.

This is where many parents get stuck. Motivation is important, but it's not enough. Change requires a plan. Your teen needs to move from "I want to" to "I'm doing it." This chapter shows you how to support that transition.

15.1 Recognizing Readiness

Before moving to action planning, you need to assess your teen's actual readiness. Just because they say they want to change doesn't mean they're ready to change.

Remember DARN CAT from section 5.2? The first four (DARN) are preparatory change talk. Desire, Ability, Reasons, Need. These show your teen is thinking about change.

The last three (CAT) are mobilizing change talk. Commitment, Activation, Taking Steps. These show they're ready to actually do something.

Listen for the shift from "I should" to "I will." From "It would be better if" to "I'm going to."

Preparatory change talk sounds like:

- "I really need to get more organized."
- "It would be good if I could bring my grades up."
- "I want my parents to trust me more."

Mobilizing change talk sounds like:

- "I'm going to start using a planner."
- "I will turn in all my assignments this week."
- "I'm ready to show them I can be responsible."

If your teen is still in preparatory mode, keep using the MI skills from earlier chapters. Explore their values, develop discrepancy, elicit more change talk. Don't rush to planning.

If they're showing mobilizing change talk, it's time to help them create a plan.

Here's how Isabella recognized readiness with her daughter Sofia, 16, about screen time. They'd been having conversations for weeks about Sofia wanting to reduce her phone use.

Sofia: "I'm actually going to do it this time. I'm putting my phone in the kitchen at 10 every night."

Isabella heard the shift. Not "I should" or "maybe I'll try." But "I'm going to" and "I'm putting." This was commitment language.

Isabella: "You sound really determined. What's different this time?"

Sofia: "I'm just done feeling like crap all the time from staying up late scrolling. I want to actually get sleep."

Isabella: "So you're ready to make a real change."

Sofia: "Yeah. I need help figuring out how to actually make it stick though."

That's the invitation to move into planning.

15.2 Collaborative Goal Setting

When your teen is ready for action, resist the urge to take over and create the plan for them. The plan has to be theirs or they won't follow it.

Collaborative goal setting means you help them articulate specific, achievable goals through questions and reflection.

Use the SMART framework (Specific, Measurable, Achievable, Relevant, Time-bound), but don't make it formulaic or boring.

Moving from vague to specific:

Vague: "I want to do better in school." Specific: "I want to bring my English grade from a D to a C by the end of the semester."

Vague: "I'm going to exercise more." Specific: "I'm going to run three times a week for 20 minutes."

Help your teen get specific through questions:

- "What would 'doing better' actually look like?"
- "How will you know if you've succeeded?"
- "What's a realistic target?"

Making goals achievable:

Too big: "I'm never going to use my phone before bed again." Achievable: "I'm going to put my phone away by 10 p.m. on school nights."

Too big: "I'm going to get straight As." Achievable: "I'm going to turn in all my homework on time and ask for help when I don't understand something."

If your teen sets unrealistic goals, gently reality-check: "That's ambitious. What would make it more manageable?" "Going from zero exercise to working out every day is a big jump. What might be a good starting point?"

Keeping goals relevant:

Connect goals back to their values (remember Chapter 7.0): "How does bringing up your grade connect to what's important to you?" "What will improving your sleep do for you?"

When goals align with personal values, motivation stays strong.

Here's how Marcus and his son Jamal, 15, worked on collaborative goal setting around video games.

Marcus: "So you've said you want to cut back on gaming. What would that actually look like?"

Jamal: "I don't know. Maybe like two hours a day instead of six?"

Marcus: "That's a big reduction. What makes you think two hours is the right amount?"

Jamal: "Well, I'd still get to play, but I'd have time for other stuff too."

Marcus: "Like what?"

Jamal: "I want to get back into basketball. And I need more time for homework."

Marcus: "So two hours of gaming leaves room for basketball and homework. How will you track the two hours?"

Jamal: "I could set a timer on my phone."

Marcus: "And what happens when the timer goes off but you're in the middle of something?"

Jamal: "I finish that match, then I'm done."

Marcus: "So the goal is: two hours of gaming on school days, with a timer. Finish the current match when time's up, then stop. That sound right?"

Jamal: "Yeah."

Notice Marcus didn't tell Jamal what his goal should be. He helped Jamal think it through and make it concrete.

15.3 Creating Action Plans

A goal without a plan is just a wish. Your teen needs specific steps for how they'll achieve their goal.

The **action plan** should include:

- Specific behaviors they'll do
- When they'll do them
- What might get in the way
- How they'll handle obstacles
- Who can support them

Use questions to help them develop the plan:

"What's the first step?" "When will you do that?" "What might get in the way?" "How will you handle it if that happens?" "Who can help you with this?"

Here's what an action plan conversation looks like. Elena is helping her daughter Camila, 15, create a plan for improving her math grade.

Elena: "Okay, so the goal is bringing your math grade from a D to a C. What's your plan for making that happen?"

Camila: "I need to do my homework every day and study for tests."

Elena: "Good start. Let's get more specific. When will you do homework?"

Camila: "After school?"

Elena: "What time after school?"

Camila: "Like, 4 to 5?"

Elena: "Where will you do it?"

Camila: "At the kitchen table, I guess."

Elena: "Okay. So 4 to 5, kitchen table, math homework. What might get in the way of that?"

Camila: "If I have volleyball practice, I won't be home until 5:30."

Elena: "So on volleyball days, what's the plan?"

Camila: "I do homework from 6 to 7 instead."

Elena: "And what about days when you're really stuck on something? What's your plan then?"

Camila: "I could text my friend Aisha. She's good at math."

Elena: "What if she can't help?"

Camila: "I could ask the teacher during study hall."

Elena: "Great. So you have backup plans. What about studying for tests? How will that work?"

Camila: "I should start studying a week before instead of the night before."

144

Elena: "How much time each day?"

Camila: "Maybe 30 minutes?"

Elena: "When?"

Camila: "After I do my regular homework."

Notice how Elena kept asking questions to make the plan more concrete. By the end, Camila had specific times, places, and backup strategies.

15.4 Supporting Small Steps

Big goals are overwhelming. Your teen is more likely to succeed if they break the goal into small, manageable steps.

Think of it like climbing stairs instead of trying to leap to the top floor. Each small step builds confidence and momentum.

Breaking down goals:

Big goal: "I'm going to get organized." Small steps:

- Week 1: Get a planner and write down all assignments
- Week 2: Check planner every morning and evening
- Week 3: Add time estimates for how long tasks will take
- Week 4: Plan out study time for the whole week

Big goal: "I'm going to stop vaping." Small steps:

- Days 1-3: Track when and why you vape (awareness)
- Days 4-7: Delay vaping by 10 minutes when you get the urge
- Week 2: Cut vaping in half
- Week 3: Only vape at specific times
- Week 4: Stop completely

Your role is to:

- Help them identify small, achievable first steps
- Celebrate each step completed
- Adjust the plan if steps are too big
- Encourage persistence when they stumble

Chen's son Wei, 14, wanted to improve his sleep schedule. The goal was going to bed by 10 p.m. He'd been going to bed around 1 a.m.

Chen helped him break it down into small steps:

Week 1: Go to bed by 12:30 Week 2: Go to bed by 12:00 Week 3: Go to bed by 11:30 Week 4: Go to bed by 11:00 Week 5: Go to bed by 10:30 Week 6: Go to bed by 10:00

Moving bedtime back by 30 minutes each week felt manageable. If Chen had pushed for 10 p.m. immediately, Wei probably would have failed and given up.

By week four, Wei was actually falling asleep earlier naturally because his body adjusted. He hit the 10 p.m. goal ahead of schedule.

Small steps work because they build **self-efficacy**. Each success proves "I can do this." That confidence carries forward to the next step.

15.5 Handling Setbacks

Your teen will have setbacks. They'll miss a day, break a commitment, or slide back into old patterns. This is completely normal. Change is rarely linear.

Your response to setbacks matters enormously. If you say "I told you so" or "See, you can't do it," you reinforce their sense of failure and kill their motivation.

If you respond with curiosity and problem-solving, setbacks become learning opportunities.

When setbacks happen:

Don't say:

- "I knew this wouldn't work."
- "You never follow through on anything."
- "Why did you even bother trying?"
- "This is exactly what I said would happen."

Do say:

- "What happened?"

- "What got in the way?"
- "What did you learn from this?"
- "What would help next time?"

Treat the setback as data, not as failure.

Here's how Diego handled it when his daughter Camila, 15, broke her commitment to limit screen time.

They'd agreed on two hours of phone time per day. For three days, Camila stuck to it. On day four, she was on her phone for five hours.

Diego's first instinct was frustration. They'd made an agreement. She'd broken it already. But he used MI instead.

Diego: "I noticed yesterday you were on your phone a lot more than the two hours we agreed on. What happened?"

Camila: "I don't know. I just lost track of time."

Diego: "Okay. So tracking time was the issue?"

Camila: "Yeah. And also, my friends were having drama in the group chat and I couldn't stop checking it."

Diego: "So two things got in the way: not tracking time well, and the pull of the drama. What would help with the time tracking piece?"

Camila: "I could set an alarm for when two hours is up."

Diego: "That might work. What about the group chat pull?"

Camila: "I don't know. When stuff is happening, it's hard to put the phone down."

Diego: "I get that. What if instead of trying to resist checking during drama, you planned for it? Like, you know drama happens. What if on those days, you gave yourself permission to go over, but you made up for it the next day?"

Camila: "So like, if I use three hours one day, I only use one the next?"

Diego: "Something like that. Does that feel more realistic?"

147

Camila: "Yeah, actually."

Diego helped Camila learn from the setback without shaming her. They adjusted the plan to be more realistic. That's how you build resilience.

15.6 Celebrating Progress

As your teen makes progress, celebrate it. Not with big rewards or over-the-top praise, but with genuine recognition of their effort and success.

Effective celebration:

- Notices specific progress: "You've done your homework on time three days in a row."
- Highlights effort and strategy: "I noticed you started studying earlier this week instead of cramming."
- Connects to their goals: "How does it feel to be following through on what you said you'd do?"

Ineffective celebration:

- Generic praise: "Good job!"
- Makes it about you: "I'm so proud of you!"
- Focuses only on outcomes: "You got an A!"

Remember from section 4.2, affirmations are more powerful than praise. Notice and name what you see.

"You set a goal and you're doing it. That takes real discipline." "I see you handling obstacles instead of giving up. That's growth." "You're proving to yourself that you can do hard things."

Jennifer's daughter Kayla, 16, had been working on managing anxiety. She'd set a goal of facing situations that made her anxious instead of avoiding them.

After a month, she'd gone to three social events she normally would have skipped. Jennifer celebrated this way:

Jennifer: "Kayla, I want to acknowledge something. A month ago, you set a goal of facing your anxiety instead of avoiding it. You've been to three events since then that you would have normally skipped. That's huge. How does it feel?"

Kayla: "Scary. But also kind of proud, I guess."

Jennifer: "You should feel proud. You're doing something really hard. What's made the difference?"

Kayla: "I don't know. Just making myself do it, I guess. And it's not as bad as I think it's going to be."

Jennifer: "That's a big insight. The anticipation is worse than the reality."

Kayla: "Yeah."

This conversation reinforced Kayla's progress and helped her recognize what was working. That's the power of thoughtful celebration.

15.7 Putting It Together

Moving from conversation to action requires recognizing when your teen is ready, helping them set specific goals, creating concrete action plans, supporting small steps, handling setbacks without judgment, and celebrating progress along the way.

You're not doing it for them. You're supporting them as they do it themselves. The plan is theirs. The follow-through is theirs. The success is theirs.

Your role is asking good questions, helping them problem-solve obstacles, staying curious when things don't go as planned, and noticing when they're making progress.

This is how lasting change happens. Not through lectures or consequences, but through your teen developing their own plan and proving to themselves they can follow through.

The next chapter addresses a challenge many parents face: getting on the same page with co-parents or stepparents.

Chapter 16.0: MI for Co-Parents

You've committed to using MI with your teen. Your co-parent hasn't. They still yell, threaten consequences, and impose rules without discussion. Your teen plays you against each other. Nothing is consistent across households. The whole thing feels like a disaster.

Co-parenting is hard enough without adding different parenting philosophies to the mix. This chapter shows you how to use MI principles with your co-parent and create enough consistency to make it work.

16.1 Getting on the Same Page

You can't force your co-parent to use MI. You can only control your own approach. But you can invite collaboration using the same MI principles you use with your teen.

Start by understanding their perspective, not by trying to convert them.

"I've been learning about a different approach to parenting teens. I'm curious what your thoughts are on how we're handling things right now. What's working? What's not?"

Notice this isn't "You're doing it wrong and I have a better way." It's genuinely curious exploration.

Your co-parent might have valid concerns about MI:

- "Sounds too permissive"
- "Teens need firm boundaries"
- "Talking doesn't work with our kid"
- "I don't have time for all that conversation"

Reflect these concerns without defending MI: "You're worried this approach is too soft." "You think structure and consequences are what our teen needs." "You've tried talking and it didn't work."

Then explore: "What's your goal with the way you're parenting right now?" "What would you like to be different?" "What matters most to you in how we parent?"

150

Often, you and your co-parent have the same goals (responsible teen, good relationship, positive outcomes) but different strategies. Focus on shared goals first.

Marcus and his ex-wife Lisa had very different parenting styles. Marcus was learning MI. Lisa was traditional, authoritarian. Their son Andre, 16, was caught in the middle.

Marcus approached Lisa with curiosity instead of criticism:

Marcus: "Lisa, can we talk about how we're handling Andre? I feel like we're not on the same page and it's confusing for him."

Lisa: "Because you let him do whatever he wants at your house."

Marcus: "You see my approach as too lenient." (Reflection)

Lisa: "It is. He needs rules. Structure."

Marcus: "Rules and structure are important to you. What's the goal of that?"

Lisa: "So he learns responsibility. So he doesn't end up screwing up his life."

Marcus: "We both want him to be responsible and make good choices. We agree on that."

Lisa: "Right."

Marcus: "I think we're trying to get to the same place different ways. Can we talk about finding some middle ground?"

By focusing on shared goals, Marcus created opening for collaboration.

16.2 Using MI With Your Co-Parent

The same MI skills work with co-parents as with teens: open questions, reflections, affirmations, summaries.

Use open questions to understand their thinking: "What's your concern about the curfew I suggested?" "Help me understand your thinking on consequences." "What would work better from your perspective?"

Reflect what you hear: "You're frustrated that our approaches are so different." "You worry that being less strict will backfire." "It sounds like you feel I'm undermining you."

Affirm when possible: "I appreciate that you're consistent with rules. That's valuable." "You really care about him learning responsibility." "Thank you for being willing to have this conversation."

Summarize to ensure understanding: "So if I'm hearing you right, you're okay with some flexibility on screen time, but you want us both to enforce homework first. And you'd like us to check in weekly about how it's going. Is that right?"

When you use MI with your co-parent, you model the collaborative approach you want them to use with your teen.

16.3 Handling Rule Disagreements

You and your co-parent will disagree about rules. That's inevitable. The question is how you handle it.

Unhelpful approaches:

- Undermining each other in front of the teen
- Letting the teen play you against each other
- Refusing to compromise
- Making unilateral decisions

MI approach:

- Discuss disagreements privately
- Find areas of agreement first
- Negotiate compromises
- Present a united front to the teen (even if imperfect)

When you disagree about a specific rule:

Focus on underlying concerns, not positions: Not: "Curfew should be 10 p.m." vs. "Curfew should be midnight." But: "What are we both worried about with curfew?" (Safety, sleep, responsibility)

Look for both/and solutions: "What if weeknight curfew is 10, weekend is 11, with flexibility for special events?"

Use provisional agreements: "Let's try this for a month and see how it goes. Then we revisit."

Prioritize the relationship: "I know we see this differently. What matters most is we're both in his life and working together. Can we find something we can both live with?"

Diego and his ex-wife had different views on their son Miguel's, 15, phone use. Diego wanted limits. His ex thought Miguel should self-regulate.

They used MI to find middle ground:

Diego: "I know we disagree about phone rules. What's your thinking on why he should self-regulate?"

Ex: "He needs to learn to manage himself. If we control everything, he won't develop that skill."

Diego: "Self-regulation is the goal. I agree with that. My concern is he's not there yet. He's on his phone until 2 a.m., missing school, grades are dropping."

Ex: "Okay, so you see current behavior as evidence he needs more structure."

Diego: "Right. What if we met in the middle? Some structure to support him developing self-regulation, not to control him forever."

Ex: "Like what?"

Diego: "What if we both require phone in the kitchen by midnight on school nights? Not because we're being controlling, but because we're helping him succeed while he builds better habits."

Ex: "And if he does it consistently?"

Diego: "Then we back off. We're helping him build the skill, not controlling him permanently."

Ex: "Okay. I can agree to that."

By focusing on shared goals (self-regulation, Miguel's success) and finding middle ground, they created a workable compromise.

16.4 Consistency Versus Flexibility

Perfect consistency across households is impossible. Your homes are different. You have different partners, schedules, and circumstances. Trying to make everything identical creates stress without much benefit.

Instead, aim for **consistency in values and core rules**, with flexibility in how they're implemented.

Core consistency (things to align on):

- Safety rules (no drinking and driving, where they can go)
- School expectations (homework gets done, attendance matters)
- Respect (basic courtesy required in both homes)
- Consequences for serious issues (substance use, legal trouble)

Acceptable flexibility (things that can vary):

- Specific chore expectations
- Exact curfew times
- Screen time limits
- House rules about food, guests, etc.

Your teen can handle different expectations in different places. They do it all the time (school rules vs. home rules vs. grandparents' rules). What they can't handle is parents undermining each other or constantly fighting.

Jennifer and her ex had different household styles. His was structured and traditional. Hers was more relaxed. Their daughter Kayla, 16, managed fine because core expectations were consistent.

Both parents expected:

- Homework completed
- Respectful communication
- Checking in about plans
- Bedtime that allowed adequate sleep

But implementation varied:

- Dad's house: strict 10 p.m. bedtime, assigned chores, limited screens
- Mom's house: flexible bedtime if tired, collaborative chore approach, screen limits by agreement

Kayla knew what to expect at each house. The consistency in values with flexibility in style worked for their family.

16.5 Stepparent Challenges

Stepparents face unique challenges. You're trying to parent someone else's child, often without the history or authority that comes with being a biological parent. MI is especially useful here.

Common stepparent struggles:

- Teen doesn't see you as a "real" parent
- Bio parent undermines your authority
- You feel like an outsider
- Teen resents your presence
- Discipline feels impossible

MI approach for stepparents:

Build relationship before rules: Focus on connection first. Spend time together without being the enforcer. Learn about their interests. Be genuinely curious about their life.

"Tell me about your soccer team." "What are you into lately?" "Help me understand what this game is about."

Collaborate with bio parent: Support the bio parent's lead rather than trying to be a parent yourself, especially early on.

"Your dad and I talked, and he wants you to..." "Your mom asked me to remind you..."

Use MI to understand their perspective: "This living situation must be weird for you. What's that like?" "How do you feel about me being here?" "What would make this easier?"

Respect their autonomy: Don't push closeness they're not ready for. Let the relationship develop naturally.

"I know I'm not your parent. I'm not trying to replace your mom. I'm just trying to be someone who supports you."

Priya married Chen, who had a 15-year-old daughter, Mei. Mei was polite but distant. Priya felt like she didn't belong.

Instead of trying to be Mei's mom, Priya used MI to build a relationship:

Priya: "Mei, I know this whole situation is probably weird for you, me being here. I'm curious how it feels from your side."

Mei: (shrugging) "It's fine."

Priya: "Fine doesn't always mean actually fine. If it's weird or hard, that's okay to say."

Mei: "I mean, it's just different. I'm used to it being me and Dad."

Priya: "That makes sense. You've had a lot of change. I'm not trying to be your mom or replace anyone. I'm just trying to be someone who's here and cares about you."

Mei: "Okay."

Priya: "If there are things that would make this easier, you can tell me. Or tell your dad and he can tell me."

Mei: "Okay."

This conversation didn't create instant closeness. But it opened the door. Priya respected Mei's space while making it clear she was open to connection when Mei was ready.

Over time, as Priya consistently showed up without pushing, Mei softened. Two years later, they had a real relationship.

16.6 United Front Strategies

Even when you disagree with your co-parent, present a united front to your teen. This doesn't mean fake agreement. It means respectful collaboration.

In front of your teen: "Your dad and I talked about this. We have different views, but here's what we agreed on..." "Your mom thinks X, I think Y, so we're meeting in the middle with Z." "We're going to try this approach for now. If it's not working, we'll revisit together."

Never in front of your teen: "I think this rule is stupid but your father insists." "I'd let you, but your mom won't." "Your dad doesn't know what he's talking about."

Undermining your co-parent teaches your teen to disrespect both of you and to manipulate the situation.

When you genuinely disagree and can't find compromise:

"Your dad and I see this differently. At his house, the rule is X. At my house, it's Y. I know that's confusing. It's not ideal. But we both love you and we're both trying our best."

Honesty with your teen about imperfect co-parenting is better than pretending to agree.

16.7 Moving Forward

Co-parenting with MI means using the same collaborative approach with your co-parent that you use with your teen. Understand their perspective. Find shared goals. Look for both/and solutions. Prioritize the relationship.

Perfect consistency isn't possible or necessary. What matters is core values alignment and respectful collaboration, even when you disagree.

If you're the only one using MI, keep using it. Your teen benefits from experiencing collaborative partnership in at least one home. Over time, your co-parent may see it working and become more open.

And if co-parenting is truly high-conflict and unworkable, focus on what you control: your relationship with your teen and your parenting in your home.

The next chapter addresses adapting MI for neurodivergent teens with ADHD, autism, or other differences.

Chapter 17.0: Neurodivergent Teens and MI

Your autistic teen doesn't understand why you're asking questions instead of just telling them what you want. Your ADHD teen forgets the plan you collaboratively created five minutes after you finish discussing it. Your neurodivergent teen needs clear, direct communication, not reflective listening.

MI works beautifully with neurodivergent teens, but it requires adaptation. This chapter shows you how.

17.1 Why Partnership Matters More

For neurodivergent teens, the MI principle of partnership (remember section 2.4) is even more critical than for neurotypical teens.

Neurodivergent teens experience being told they're doing things wrong constantly. School doesn't fit their brain. Social expectations feel arbitrary. They're given executive function tasks they genuinely struggle with, then blamed for not trying hard enough.

By the time they're teenagers, many neurodivergent kids have internalized the message that they're broken, difficult, or wrong.

MI offers something different: a framework where you're collaborators, not adversaries. Where their perspective matters. Where challenges are problems to solve together, not character flaws to fix.

This matters for every teen. For neurodivergent teens, it's essential.

Aisha's son Hassan, 15, had ADHD. School had been a nightmare since kindergarten. Every teacher told him to focus, sit still, try harder. By high school, Hassan was convinced he was stupid and defective.

When Aisha learned about MI, she changed how she talked to Hassan:

Instead of: "You need to focus on your homework." She said: "What gets in the way when you're trying to do homework?"

Instead of: "Why can't you just remember your assignments?" She said: "Your brain works differently than the way school is set up. What tools would help you track assignments better?"

This shift, acknowledging that Hassan's challenges were about brain difference not character failure, changed everything. Hassan started seeing himself as someone with specific needs, not someone who was fundamentally wrong.

17.2 Adapting for Executive Function

Many neurodivergent teens (especially those with ADHD, autism, or learning disabilities) have executive function challenges. They struggle with planning, organizing, remembering, and following through.

Standard MI assumes certain capabilities: your teen can track a conversation, remember what they committed to, and execute on plans. For teens with executive function challenges, you need to provide more structure and support.

Adaptations:

Write things down: After conversations about goals or plans, write them down together. Visual reminders help.

"Let's write out the plan so you can refer back to it."

Break things into smaller steps: What seems like one task to you might be five tasks for them.

Not: "Clean your room." But: "Step 1: Put clothes in hamper. Step 2: Put books on shelf. Step 3: Clear desk surface."

Use external supports: Phone reminders, visual schedules, checklists, apps. Don't expect them to remember through willpower.

Check in more frequently: Weekly check-ins on plans, not monthly. Their working memory might not hold the plan that long.

Celebrate tiny wins: Executive function challenges mean every small success required genuine effort.

Chen's son Wei, 14, had ADHD. They'd created a plan for homework. Wei was committed. But three days later, he'd completely forgotten the plan existed.

Chen adapted:

- Wrote the plan on a whiteboard in Wei's room
- Set phone reminders for homework time
- Checked in daily for the first week ("What's your plan for homework today?")
- Broke assignments into 15-minute chunks with breaks

With these supports, Wei could actually follow through. Without them, he wasn't being defiant. He genuinely couldn't hold the plan in his mind.

17.3 ADHD-Specific Strategies

ADHD brains work differently. They struggle with motivation for non-preferred tasks, have poor time awareness, get overwhelmed easily, and are highly distractible.

MI with ADHD teens:

Harness hyperfocus: ADHD teens can focus intensely on things they find interesting. Use this.

"What makes something interesting enough that you can focus on it?" "How can we make this more engaging for your brain?"

Address the motivation piece directly: ADHD brains need more immediate rewards than neurotypical brains.

"What would make this feel less painful?" "What reward would you like after completing this?"

Accept that willpower won't work: ADHD isn't a willpower problem. Scaffold the environment instead.

"What would make it impossible for you to get distracted?" (Phone in another room, specific workspace, body doubling)

Use body doubling: Many ADHD people work better with someone else present, even if that person isn't helping.

"Would it help if I sat nearby while you work?"

Time awareness strategies: Clocks don't work for ADHD brains. Use timers, alarms, and time limits.

"Let's work for 20 minutes, then take a break."

Diego's daughter Camila, 14, had ADHD. Homework was a nightly battle. Using these strategies helped:

Diego: "What makes homework so hard for you?"

Camila: "It's boring. And I can't stay focused."

Diego: "Okay. So we need to make it less boring and set you up for focus. What would help with the boring part?"

Camila: "I don't know. Music?"

Diego: "Let's try it. What about focus?"

Camila: "If my phone isn't in the room, that helps."

Diego: "Okay. Phone stays with me. What else?"

Camila: "Maybe if I did like 15 minutes, then a break, then 15 more?"

Diego: "We can do that. I'll sit in the kitchen while you work. Not hovering, just there. Would that help or make it worse?"

Camila: "That might actually help."

With phone away, music on, 15-minute chunks, and Diego nearby, Camila could focus. The structure supported her brain's needs.

17.4 Understanding Autistic Differences

Autistic teens process communication differently. What feels collaborative to you might feel confusing to them. What feels like partnership might feel like you're being indirect and unclear.

Adaptations for autistic teens:

Be more direct: "I noticed you've been staying up really late. I'm concerned about how tired you are. I'd like us to figure out a better sleep schedule together."

Not: "How have you been sleeping?" (Too vague)

Explain the why clearly: Autistic people often need logical reasons, not just "because I said so."

"I want you home by 10 because I worry about your safety late at night, and I sleep better when I know you're home."

Respect sensory needs: If your teen says lights are too bright or sounds are too loud, believe them. Sensory issues are real, not manipulation.

"What would make this environment more comfortable for you?"

Understand social communication differences: Eye contact might be painful. Tone of voice might not convey what you think it does. They might interpret your words literally.

"I'm going to be direct because that's usually easier: Here's what I need from you..."

Allow for processing time: Autistic brains often need more time to process information and formulate responses.

"Take your time thinking about this. We can talk more tomorrow."

Respect special interests: Deep interests aren't obsessions to eliminate. They're sources of joy and regulation.

"I know you need time for [special interest]. Let's figure out how to make sure you get that while also handling responsibilities."

Marcus's son Andre, 16, was autistic. Marcus had been using MI but Andre seemed confused by it. Marcus realized he needed to adapt.

Instead of: "How are you feeling about school?" He said: "I've noticed your grades are lower this semester. I'm concerned. Do you know what's going on?"

Instead of: "What do you think we should do about curfew?" He said: "Your current curfew is 10 p.m. You want it later. I'm concerned about safety and sleep. Let's figure out a specific time that addresses both."

Being more direct and explicit helped Andre engage with the conversation. MI still worked. It just needed to be more concrete and clear.

17.5 Case Study: MI with Autism

Let's look at a complete example of using adapted MI with an autistic teen.

Background: Elena's daughter Sofia, 15, is autistic. She has good language skills but struggles with social situations and sensory issues. Sofia has been melting down frequently after school. Elena wants to understand what's wrong and help.

Elena: "Sofia, I've noticed you've been having meltdowns after school most days this week. I want to understand what's going on. Are you okay talking about it?" (Direct, asking permission)

Sofia: "School is too loud."

Elena: "The noise level at school is overwhelming for you." (Reflection)

Sofia: "Yes. The cafeteria is the worst. Everyone's talking and the chairs scraping and the fluorescent lights buzzing. It's too much."

Elena: "So it's not just noise. It's also the lights." (Clarifying)

Sofia: "All of it. By the end of the day I can't think anymore."

Elena: "You're overwhelmed by sensory input all day, and by the time you get home, you're completely overloaded." (Reflection showing understanding)

Sofia: "Yes."

Elena: "That sounds really hard. What would help?" (Open question)

Sofia: "I don't know. Not going to school?" (Half joking)

Elena: "School's not optional, but we can figure out ways to make it more manageable. What helps when you're feeling overwhelmed?" (Reframing, focusing on solutions)

Sofia: "Being in my room with the lights off and my headphones on."

Elena: "Okay. So when you get home, you need quiet and dark to recover. What if we made that part of your routine? You get home, go straight to your room for 30 minutes to decompress. Then we do homework or whatever else needs to happen." (Collaborative solution)

Sofia: "That would help."

Elena: "What about during school? Is there anywhere you can go when it gets too much?"

Sofia: "The library is quieter."

Elena: "Could you ask to go to the library during lunch instead of the cafeteria?"

Sofia: "Maybe. I'd have to bring my lunch."

Elena: "We can do that. Let's try it next week. Library at lunch, quiet room time when you get home. See if that helps with the meltdowns." (Concrete plan)

Sofia: "Okay."

Elena used adapted MI: direct questions, concrete solutions, respect for sensory needs, collaborative problem-solving. Sofia felt understood and got support she needed.

17.6 Resources and Support

Parenting neurodivergent teens requires understanding their specific needs. Resources that can help:

For ADHD:

- CHADD (Children and Adults with Attention-Deficit/Hyperactivity Disorder)
- Books like "Taking Charge of ADHD" by Russell Barkley

- Executive function coaching
- Medication management with a psychiatrist if appropriate

For Autism:

- Autistic self-advocates' writing and resources
- Books like "Uniquely Human" by Barry Prizant
- Social skills groups (only if teen wants them)
- Occupational therapy for sensory needs

For Learning Disabilities:

- Educational advocacy organizations
- Neuropsychological evaluation
- IEP or 504 accommodations at school
- Specialized tutoring

Remember, the goal isn't to make your neurodivergent teen neurotypical. It's to support them in building skills, using accommodations, and thriving as their authentic self.

17.7 Key Takeaways

MI works beautifully with neurodivergent teens when adapted for their specific needs. Partnership matters even more because these teens experience being told they're wrong constantly.

For executive function challenges, provide external supports rather than expecting internal willpower. For ADHD, structure the environment for success. For autism, be more direct and concrete while respecting sensory and communication differences.

The core MI spirit (partnership, acceptance, compassion, evocation) remains the same. The implementation gets more specific and concrete for neurodivergent brains.

The final chapter troubleshoots common problems and helps you adjust MI when it's not working.

Chapter 18.0: Troubleshooting MI

You've tried everything in this book. You've used OARS, developed discrepancy, rolled with resistance. And it's still not working. Your teen won't talk, or they talk but don't change, or you keep losing your temper and ruining the MI approach.

This chapter helps you troubleshoot when MI isn't working and adapt it for different situations and personalities.

18.1 Common Roadblocks

Roadblock 1: You're trying too hard

When you first learn MI, it's easy to overdo it. You reflect everything. Every conversation becomes therapy. You're so focused on technique that you lose natural connection.

Solution: Use MI strategically, not constantly. Save it for important conversations. In casual moments, just be a parent. Chat normally. Let technique fade into the background.

Roadblock 2: Your teen sees through it

"Why are you talking like that?" or "Are you reading from a script?" Your teen notices you're using a technique and it feels manipulative.

Solution: Acknowledge it honestly. "You're right, I am trying a different approach. I realized our old way of talking wasn't working. I'm trying to actually listen instead of just lecturing. Bear with me while I figure this out."

Roadblock 3: The timing is wrong

You're trying to have important MI conversations when your teen is tired, hungry, stressed, or already upset.

Solution: Ask if now is a good time. "Can we talk about something important? Is now good, or would later be better?" Respect the answer.

Roadblock 4: You're rushing to solutions

You ask two questions, then jump to advice. You haven't actually understood their perspective yet.

Solution: Spend more time in exploration. Ask more questions. Reflect more. Be genuinely curious. Stay in listening mode longer before moving to problem-solving.

Roadblock 5: You have an agenda

You're using MI to get them to agree with what you already decided. They sense this and resist.

Solution: Get honest about your agenda. If there's a non-negotiable, say so upfront. If it's truly collaborative, let go of the outcome you want and be open to their ideas.

18.2 When They Won't Talk

Some teens are silent. They give one-word answers, shrug, or refuse to engage no matter how good your questions are.

Why teens shut down:

- Previous conversations have been punitive
- They don't trust you yet
- They're protecting themselves
- They genuinely don't know how they feel
- Talking isn't their communication style

What to try:

Parallel activities: Some teens talk more easily when doing something else. Drive in the car. Throw a ball. Cook together. The activity takes pressure off eye contact and direct conversation.

"Want to come to the store with me? We can talk on the way if you want."

Written communication: Some teens express themselves better in writing. Try texts or notes.

"If talking feels hard, you could text me what's going on."

Wait it out: Sometimes silence means they're thinking. Don't fill every pause. Give them space to respond.

Acknowledge the pattern: "I notice when I try to talk to you about serious stuff, you shut down. What's that about?"

Lower stakes first: Build connection through easier conversations before tackling hard topics.

Accept some teens won't talk: Not every teen is going to open up verbally. Focus on maintaining connection through other means.

Jennifer's son David, 15, would not talk. Every attempt at conversation got shrugs or "I don't know."

Jennifer tried parallel activities. She'd ask him to help with dinner. While chopping vegetables together, she'd ask simple questions:

"How was practice?" "Anything interesting happen today?"

Not heavy topics. Just connection. Gradually, David started sharing more. The activity made it easier than sitting face-to-face.

Six months later, when something serious came up, David actually talked to her. The foundation of easier conversations made the hard one possible.

18.3 Repairing After Losing It

You're going to lose your temper. You'll yell, say something you regret, impose consequences you didn't mean, or abandon MI completely in the moment. This is normal.

What matters is how you repair it.

How to repair:

Apologize sincerely: "I lost my temper and yelled at you. That wasn't okay. I'm sorry."

Not: "I'm sorry but you..." (That's not an apology.)

Take responsibility: "I handled that badly. I was frustrated and I didn't manage my emotions well."

Don't blame them: "You pushed my buttons" is not accountability. Your emotions are your responsibility.

Explain what you'll do differently: "Next time I feel that frustrated, I'm going to take a break before we talk. I don't want to yell at you like that again."

Ask what would help: "How can I make this right?"

Return to the issue when calm: "I still need to talk about what happened. Can we try again when we're both calm?"

Diego blew up at his daughter Camila over a messy room. He yelled that she was lazy and irresponsible. As soon as he said it, he knew he'd crossed a line.

An hour later, Diego went to Camila's room:

Diego: "Camila, I owe you an apology. I got really angry and I said things I shouldn't have said. You're not lazy or irresponsible. I was frustrated about the room, but the way I handled it was wrong. I'm sorry."

Camila: "Okay."

Diego: "The room still needs to be dealt with. But I'd like to talk about it differently. When you're ready."

Camila: "Okay."

The repair didn't fix everything instantly. But it showed Camila that Diego could acknowledge mistakes and take responsibility. That matters.

18.4 Cultural Considerations

MI was developed in Western, individualistic cultures. It emphasizes autonomy, individual choice, and verbal expression. These values don't translate perfectly to all cultural contexts.

Adaptations for different cultural contexts:

Collectivist cultures: Some cultures prioritize family and community over individual autonomy. MI's emphasis on teen autonomy might feel wrong.

Adaptation: Frame autonomy within family context. "What's best for you and for our family?" "How can we honor both your needs and our family values?"

High-context communication cultures: Some cultures communicate indirectly. Asking direct questions feels rude or invasive.

Adaptation: Use more observation and gentle inquiry. "I've noticed..." instead of "Tell me..."

Hierarchical cultures: Some cultures have strong parent authority. Collaborative conversation might feel like undermining parental role.

Adaptation: Maintain appropriate hierarchy while seeking input. "I'm making this decision, but I want to hear your thoughts first."

Different emotional expression norms: Some cultures value emotional restraint. MI's focus on exploring feelings might be uncomfortable.

Adaptation: Focus more on thoughts and values, less on emotions. "What do you think about this situation?" instead of "How do you feel?"

Language considerations: For families where English isn't the primary language, translation might lose nuance.

Adaptation: Use simpler language, check understanding frequently, be patient with communication barriers.

Chen, originally from Taiwan, found some MI concepts felt culturally foreign. The emphasis on teen autonomy conflicted with his values about family respect.

He adapted MI to fit his context:

"In our family, we respect elders and we also value each person's thoughts. Help me understand your perspective on this."

"I'm your father, so ultimately I make certain decisions. But your input matters to me. What are your thoughts?"

This balanced cultural values with MI principles. Not perfect by Western MI standards, but authentic and effective for his family.

18.5 When to Get Professional Help

Sometimes the issues are bigger than MI can address. Signs you need professional help:

For your teen:

- Serious mental health concerns (depression, anxiety, suicidal thoughts)
- Substance abuse
- Violent or destructive behavior
- Complete breakdown of communication
- Academic failure despite capability
- Social isolation or withdrawal

For the family:

- You've tried MI consistently for months with no improvement
- Conflict is constant and severe
- You feel completely out of your depth
- Other family members are suffering
- You're too emotionally involved to stay calm

Types of professional help:

Individual therapy for teen: Therapist works with your teen on their issues.

Family therapy: Therapist works with the whole family on communication and dynamics.

Parent coaching: Someone helps you develop skills and strategies.

Psychiatric evaluation: If medication might be appropriate for mental health issues.

Professional help doesn't mean you failed. It means the situation needs more support than one parent using a parenting approach can provide.

18.6 Adjusting for Different Personalities

Not all teens respond to MI the same way. Adjust your approach for your teen's personality.

For the analytical teen:

- Provide logical reasons
- Use data and facts
- Let them research options
- Give them time to think before deciding

For the emotional teen:

- Spend more time with feelings
- Validate emotions thoroughly
- Connect decisions to values and relationships
- Provide emotional support alongside problem-solving

For the action-oriented teen:

- Keep conversations shorter and more focused
- Move to action planning faster
- Use concrete examples
- Let them try things and learn from experience

For the introverted teen:

- Give processing time
- Don't pressure immediate responses
- Use written communication if helpful
- Respect their need for space

For the extroverted teen:

- Let them talk through ideas out loud
- Provide social support and accountability
- Involve friends in positive ways
- Keep energy high in conversations

For the concrete thinker:

- Be very specific
- Avoid abstract concepts

- Use examples and demonstrations
- Create visible systems and plans

For the abstract thinker:

- Discuss big picture and meaning
- Connect to larger values and goals
- Allow exploration of ideas
- Don't get bogged down in excessive detail

Marcus realized his son Terrell, 17, was analytical. Emotional exploration didn't work well. But give Terrell data and logic, and he engaged completely.

Marcus adjusted:

"Research shows teens need 8-10 hours of sleep for optimal brain function. You're getting about 6. What do you think that's doing to your performance?"

This worked better for Terrell than "How do you feel about your sleep?"

18.7 Final Thoughts

MI isn't magic. It won't work perfectly every time. You'll make mistakes, lose your temper, say the wrong thing, or find that your teen just won't engage.

That's okay. Progress matters more than perfection.

Keep using the core principles: partnership, acceptance, compassion, evocation. Ask good questions. Listen more than you talk. Stay curious instead of judgmental. Help your teen find their own motivation.

When it's not working, troubleshoot. Adjust for your teen's personality, your cultural context, and the specific situation. Get professional help when needed. Repair when you mess up.

The goal isn't to be a perfect MI practitioner. The goal is to build a relationship with your teen where they feel heard, respected, and supported in becoming their own person.

You're doing hard work. Parenting teenagers is challenging for everyone. The fact that you're reading this book and trying to improve your approach shows how much you care.

Your teen is lucky to have a parent who's willing to learn, adapt, and keep trying even when it's hard.

18.8 Wrapping Up

When MI isn't working, step back and assess. Are you trying too hard? Is the timing wrong? Does it need adjustment for personality or culture? Do you need professional support?

Repair ruptures when you lose your temper. Adjust for your teen's specific personality and communication style. Use parallel activities when direct conversation doesn't work. Be patient with teens who don't open up easily.

MI is a framework, not a script. Adapt it to fit your family, your teen, and your cultural context while maintaining the core spirit of collaborative partnership.

The remaining chapters bring everything together and help you maintain MI skills long-term. You've learned the tools. Now we focus on integration and sustainability.

Chapter 19.0: Building Lifelong Skills

Your teen is 17. In a year, they'll be legally an adult. They'll make decisions about college, work, relationships, money, and health without your permission. Ready or not, adulthood is coming.

The question isn't if they'll be independent. It's how prepared they'll be when independence arrives. And here's what most parents don't realize: the way you parent now directly shapes their decision-making skills for life.

This chapter shows you how MI isn't just about getting through the teenage years. It's about building the foundation for a capable, thoughtful adult.

19.1 How MI Teaches Decisions

Traditional parenting teaches teens to follow rules. MI teaches them to make decisions.

There's a huge difference.

When you tell your teen what to do, they learn to comply or rebel. When you help them think through decisions, they learn to evaluate options, consider consequences, and make choices aligned with their values.

These are the skills they'll need at 25, 35, and 45, when you're not there to tell them what to do.

Decision-making skills MI builds:

Identifying values: Through all those conversations about what matters to them, they learn to articulate their values. This becomes their internal compass.

Evaluating options: When you ask "what are your choices here?" instead of telling them the right choice, they practice generating and evaluating options.

Considering consequences: "What do you think happens if you do that?" helps them develop consequential thinking, the ability to project forward.

Tolerating ambiguity: Not every decision has a clear right answer. MI helps teens get comfortable with uncertainty and making the best choice with imperfect information.

Learning from mistakes: When you use setbacks as learning opportunities (remember section 15.5), they develop resilience and adaptability.

Trusting themselves: Perhaps most importantly, they learn to trust their own judgment. This is the foundation of adult autonomy.

Marcus watched his son Terrell, 18, apply these skills to his college decision. Terrell had been accepted to three schools: his dream school (expensive, far away), a solid state school (affordable, closer), and a local community college (cheap, could live at home).

Marcus's instinct was to push for the affordable option. But he used MI instead.

Marcus: "You've got three good options. How are you thinking about it?"

Terrell: "I really want to go to the dream school. But I'm worried about debt."

Marcus: "So there's a conflict between what you want and what feels financially responsible."

Terrell: "Yeah. I keep going back and forth."

Marcus: "Walk me through the pros and cons of each option."

Terrell spent 30 minutes talking through each school. The location, the programs, the cost, the debt he'd graduate with, the opportunities each offered, how he felt about each place.

Marcus mostly listened and asked clarifying questions. He didn't tell Terrell what to decide.

At the end, Terrell said: "I think I'm going to do two years at community college, then transfer to the state school. I'll save money, stay closer to home while I figure things out, and still get a good degree."

This wasn't the decision Marcus would have made for him. But it was a thoughtful decision that Terrell owned completely. The process of thinking it through prepared him for the thousands of decisions he'd make in adulthood.

19.2 Preparing for Adult Life

The teenage years are a training ground for adulthood. Every challenge is an opportunity to build skills they'll need later.

Executive function skills: Planning, organizing, time management, emotional regulation. These don't develop automatically. They develop through practice with support.

Instead of managing their schedule for them, help them learn to manage it: "You've got three things due this week. How are you going to handle it?"

Financial literacy: Let them make money decisions and experience natural consequences. Give them a clothing budget and let them manage it. Let them earn money and decide how to spend or save it.

"You want those expensive shoes. You have $100 in your account. How do you want to handle this?"

Relationship skills: Help them navigate friend conflicts, dating challenges, and social situations using the skills from Chapter 11.0.

"This situation with your friend sounds really hard. What are you thinking about doing?"

Self-advocacy: Teach them to speak up for themselves. Let them make their own doctor appointments, talk to teachers about grades, resolve their own issues with coaches.

"You're upset about playing time. Have you talked to your coach? What would you say?"

Domestic skills: By 18, they should know how to cook basic meals, do laundry, clean, and handle basic home maintenance.

Not because you're their servant, but because you're preparing them for independence.

Isabella realized when her daughter Sofia, 17, was a senior that she'd done too much for her. Sofia had never done her own laundry, couldn't cook more than ramen, and had no idea how to make a doctor's appointment.

Isabella started systematically teaching these skills, using MI to make Sofia a partner in the process:

Isabella: "Next year you'll be living in a dorm. What life skills do you think you need before then?"

Sofia: "I don't know. Laundry? Cooking?"

Isabella: "Good start. What else?"

Sofia: "How to manage money, I guess. And like, adult stuff. Making appointments and paying bills."

Isabella: "Let's make a plan. Between now and when you leave, let's work on all of those. Where do you want to start?"

They created a plan where Sofia took over one new responsibility each month: January was laundry, February was meal planning and cooking twice a week, March was managing her own calendar and appointments, April was budgeting her spending money.

By the time Sofia left for college, she had the basic skills she needed. More importantly, she had confidence that she could figure things out.

19.3 College and Career Transitions

The transition to college or career is huge. Your teen is suddenly responsible for everything: schedule, homework, social life, health, money, daily decisions about sleep, food, and time management.

Many 18-year-olds crash and burn in their first semester because they've never had to manage all of this simultaneously.

How MI prepares them:

By giving them increasing autonomy during high school, you've gradually transferred responsibility. They've practiced making decisions with you as a safety net. Now they're ready to do it independently.

By teaching them to identify and solve problems, you've given them a framework for handling new challenges.

By maintaining connection through collaborative conversation, you've built a relationship where they'll come to you when they need help (not because you'll fix it, but because you'll help them think it through).

Your role during the transition:

Be available but not intrusive. Check in, but don't micromanage.

"How's it going?" not "Did you go to all your classes this week?"

When they struggle (and they will), use MI to help them problem-solve:

"Sounds like you're overwhelmed. What's the hardest part?" "What have you tried?" "What would help?"

Let them experience natural consequences. If they party instead of studying and fail a test, that's valuable learning. Don't rescue them.

But if they're genuinely struggling with mental health, or in over their head, step in with support. Know the difference between "learning from mistakes" and "drowning."

Diego's son Miguel, 18, struggled his first semester of college. His grades were terrible. He was skipping classes. Diego's first instinct was to lecture and threaten.

Instead, he used MI:

Diego: "Miguel, I got your grades. You're struggling. Talk to me about what's going on."

Miguel: "I don't know. College is harder than I thought. And I'm behind now and I don't know how to catch up."

Diego: "So you're overwhelmed and it feels like too much to fix."

Miguel: "Yeah."

Diego: "What do you think needs to happen?"

Miguel: "I need to go to class. And I need help. Like, tutoring or something."

Diego: "Those sound like good first steps. What's getting in the way of going to class?"

Miguel: "I stay up too late and then I can't wake up."

Diego: "Okay, so sleep is part of the problem. What would help with that?"

Miguel: "I need to actually go to bed at a reasonable time."

Diego: "What would it take to make that happen?"

Through this conversation, Miguel identified his own solutions. Diego's role was asking questions and showing confidence that Miguel could figure it out.

19.4 Letting Go While Connected

One of the hardest parts of parenting teens turning into adults is the letting go piece. You've spent 18 years protecting them, guiding them, making decisions for them. Now you have to step back.

But letting go doesn't mean disconnecting. It means changing the nature of the relationship.

What changes:

- You move from manager to consultant
- From decision maker to sounding board
- From authority to advisor
- From parent to parent-and-friend

What stays the same:

- You still love them fiercely
- You're still available when they need you
- You still care about their wellbeing
- The connection remains

The MI approach makes this transition easier because you've been moving in this direction all along. You've been treating them as partners, not subordinates. You've been asking instead of telling. You've been collaborative instead of authoritarian.

So when they turn 18, it's not a sudden shift. It's a continuation of the relationship you've been building.

Boundaries in adult relationships:

Your adult child makes their own decisions. Even ones you disagree with.

You can share your perspective: "Here's what I think, but it's your decision."

You can set boundaries about what you will and won't support: "I won't pay for that, but I support your right to choose it."

But you can't control them anymore. And that's as it should be.

Jennifer struggled with this when her daughter Kayla, 19, decided to take a gap year instead of going straight to college. Jennifer thought it was a mistake. She worried Kayla wouldn't ever go back to school.

But Jennifer used MI principles:

Jennifer: "I'm surprised by this decision. Help me understand your thinking."

Kayla: "I'm burned out from school. I need a break. And I want to work and save money."

Jennifer: "So you need time to recharge and you have financial goals."

Kayla: "Yeah. And honestly, I don't even know what I want to study. I think I need to figure that out before spending money on college."

Jennifer: "That makes sense. What's your plan for the year?"

Kayla: "Work full-time, save money, and figure out what I actually want to do with my life."

Jennifer: "Okay. I hear you. I have some concerns about gap years, but it's your decision. Can I share my concerns?"

Kayla: "Sure."

Jennifer: "My worry is that it's easier to stay in school momentum than to go back after a break. I've seen people get comfortable working and never return to college. How would you prevent that?"

Kayla: "I'd commit to applying during my gap year. So I'd start the following fall, not just indefinitely postpone."

Jennifer: "That addresses my concern. I support you taking this year if you commit to applying and starting the next year."

Jennifer didn't love the decision. But she respected Kayla's autonomy and shared her concerns honestly. Their relationship stayed strong because Jennifer let Kayla make her own choice.

19.5 MI With Young Adults

MI doesn't stop when your teen turns 18. The principles work beautifully with young adults, with some adaptations.

With young adults:

They have even more autonomy. You're truly a consultant now, not a parent making decisions. Your input is offered, not imposed.

The stakes are higher. They're making decisions about careers, serious relationships, money, where to live. These have long-term consequences.

They have more life experience. They know more now. Your conversations can go deeper.

The relationship is more equal. Less parent-child, more adult-to-adult.

You use MI even more lightly. A few strategic questions, reflection when they share something. You're not conducting MI sessions. You're just a good conversational partner.

Marcus's son Terrell, 22, was considering quitting his job to travel for six months. Marcus thought it was irresponsible. But Terrell was an adult.

Marcus: "Tell me about this travel idea."

Terrell: "I want to backpack through South America. I've been working for two years straight. I need an adventure."

Marcus: "So you're feeling burned out and craving something different."

Terrell: "Exactly."

Marcus: "What's your plan? How would this work financially?"

Terrell: "I've saved $10,000. That's enough for six months of budget travel."

Marcus: "And after? What's the plan for when you come back?"

Terrell: "Find another job. My field is growing, I'm not worried about finding work."

Marcus: "What about career trajectory? Does taking six months off set you back?"

Terrell: "Maybe. But I'm 22. I'd rather have the experience now than wait until I'm 40 with kids and a mortgage."

Marcus: "That's fair. I can see your reasoning. Can I share one concern?"

Terrell: "Sure."

Marcus: "My concern is that $10,000 sounds like a lot, but it can disappear fast, especially if something goes wrong. What's your backup plan if you run out of money?"

Terrell: "I'd come home early if I had to. But I've budgeted carefully. I think I'll be okay."

Marcus: "Alright. I'm not saying don't do it. I'm saying make sure you've thought through the risks."

Terrell: "I appreciate that, Dad."

Marcus didn't try to stop Terrell. He asked good questions, shared concerns, and trusted Terrell to decide. That's the MI approach with young adults.

19.6 Long Term Benefits

The benefits of MI parenting show up years later. Research on parenting styles consistently finds that authoritative parenting (warm and demanding, which MI embodies) produces the best long-term outcomes (Steinberg, 2001).

Adults raised with MI approach tend to:

Make better decisions: They've practiced decision-making with support. They know how to evaluate options and consider consequences.

Have better mental health: They've learned emotional regulation and problem-solving. They're less anxious and depressed.

Have stronger relationships: They've experienced collaborative, respectful relationships. They recreate that pattern in their own relationships.

Have higher self-esteem: They trust their own judgment because they've been treated as capable people whose perspectives matter.

Be more resilient: They've learned to handle setbacks without catastrophizing. They bounce back.

Be better parents themselves: They parent their own kids the way they were parented. The cycle continues.

Elena watched her daughter Camila, now 25, become a parent. Camila's approach to her own toddler reflected the MI principles Elena had used with her.

When the toddler melted down about something, Camila didn't yell or punish. She got curious: "You're really upset. What's going on?"

When the toddler wanted to do something unsafe, Camila explained why and offered choices: "We can't play with the outlet. That's dangerous. Would you like to play with blocks or read a book?"

Elena teared up watching it. The collaborative, respectful approach she'd worked so hard to maintain with Camila through the difficult teenage years had become Camila's natural parenting style.

That's the long game.

19.7 Looking Forward

Parenting teenagers with MI isn't easy. It takes patience, self-control, and willingness to let them make mistakes. It's often slower and more frustrating than just telling them what to do.

But it's worth it.

Years from now, you'll have an adult child who calls you for advice (not because they have to, but because they value your input). Who makes thoughtful decisions. Who handles challenges with resilience. Who has healthy relationships. Who trusts themselves.

And you'll have a relationship with them based on mutual respect and genuine connection, not obligation or guilt.

That's what MI builds. Not just compliance during the teenage years, but capability for a lifetime.

The final chapter addresses something crucial: taking care of yourself through this challenging process.

Chapter 20.0: Taking Care of Yourself

You've stayed calm through yet another argument. You've used reflective listening when you wanted to scream. You've rolled with resistance when every cell in your body wanted to just impose consequences and be done with it.

And now you're exhausted, questioning yourself, wondering if you're doing any of this right.

Here's the truth nobody tells you about parenting with MI: it's hard on you. It requires emotional regulation, patience, and self-control that sometimes feel impossible. If you don't take care of yourself, you can't sustain it.

This final chapter is about you. Your needs, your emotions, your wellbeing. Because you matter too.

20.1 Managing Your Emotions

MI asks you to stay calm and curious when your teen is pushing every button you have. That takes serious emotional management.

You can't just suppress your emotions. That leads to eventual explosion. You need strategies for actually managing what you feel.

Recognize your triggers: What specifically sets you off? Disrespect? Lying? Seeing them make choices you made and regretted? When you know your triggers, you can prepare for them.

Notice your body: Emotions show up physically before they show up in behavior. When you notice your jaw clenching, shoulders tensing, or heart racing, that's your cue to pause.

Take breaks: You don't have to respond immediately to every situation. "I need a few minutes to think about this" is a completely valid response.

Breathe: It sounds simple, but slow breathing actually calms your nervous system. Five deep breaths can shift you from reactive to responsive.

Have an outlet: Exercise, journaling, talking to friends, therapy. Find ways to process the hard emotions instead of stuffing them down.

Know when you're too activated: Sometimes you're too angry or upset to handle a conversation well. That's okay. "I'm too upset to talk about this right now. Let's talk tomorrow" maintains the relationship while protecting both of you from a destructive conversation.

Chen noticed he got most triggered when his son Wei, 16, lied. It brought up Chen's own issues about trust and respect from his childhood. Just recognizing this pattern helped.

When Chen caught Wei lying, instead of immediately exploding, he'd say: "I need some time to calm down before we talk about this. We'll discuss it tonight after dinner."

That space let Chen process his emotions, remember his goals, and approach the conversation more calmly.

20.2 Self Reflective Listening

You ask your teen to examine their thoughts and feelings. It helps to do the same for yourself.

Self-reflective listening means turning the MI skills inward. Getting curious about your own reactions, values, and patterns.

When you're upset with your teen, ask yourself:

- What am I actually feeling? (Scared? Angry? Disappointed? Worried?)
- What's underneath that feeling? (Fear they'll fail? Worry I'm failing as a parent? My own unmet needs?)
- What do I value that feels threatened? (Safety? Respect? Their success?)
- What's my part in this dynamic?

This isn't about blaming yourself. It's about self-awareness that helps you respond more effectively.

Isabella realized she got most frustrated with her daughter Sofia, 17, around achievement. Every grade, every college application, every award mattered intensely to Isabella.

When she used self-reflective listening, she recognized this was about her own regrets. Isabella had given up on her own dreams when she had kids young. She was living vicariously through Sofia's achievements.

This realization helped Isabella step back. Sofia's achievements weren't about Isabella. Sofia needed to find her own path, not fulfill Isabella's unmet ambitions.

Questions for self-reflection:

- What's really bothering me about this situation?
- Am I upset about their behavior, or about what it means about me as a parent?
- What would I tell a friend in this situation?
- Am I treating them the way I want to be treated?
- What do I need right now?

You can journal these questions, talk them through with a friend, or just think about them. The process of honest self-examination makes you a better parent.

20.3 Dealing With Outside Judgment

When you use MI, other people will judge you.

"You're too soft." "Kids need discipline." "Just take away their phone." "You're letting them walk all over you."

Friends, family, other parents, even strangers will have opinions about your parenting. Some will be directly critical. Others will subtly undermine your approach.

This is hard. You're already questioning yourself. External criticism makes it worse.

Strategies for handling judgment:

Remember your values: You chose this approach for good reasons. When you're clear about why you're parenting this way, others' opinions matter less.

You don't need to justify yourself: You can simply say, "We're doing what works for our family" and change the subject.

Set boundaries: If someone is constantly criticizing, you can say, "I've heard your concerns. I'm not going to discuss this anymore."

Find your people: Connect with other parents who share your values. Support from people who get it makes all the difference.

Trust your relationship with your teen: If your approach is strengthening your connection and helping them grow, that's what matters. Not what your mother-in-law thinks.

Remember the long game: These critics won't be there at 2 a.m. when your adult child calls you for advice because they trust and respect you. You will.

Diego got constant criticism from his father about his parenting. His father believed in strict discipline, immediate consequences, and minimal conversation. He thought Diego was ruining his kids with all the talking and collaborating.

Diego finally said: "Dad, I appreciate that you have strong opinions. We're parenting differently than you did. I'm not going to discuss it anymore. If you want a relationship with your grandkids, you need to respect how we're raising them."

It was hard. But the boundary was necessary.

20.4 Finding Your Support System

Parenting teenagers is isolating. Everyone's struggling, but nobody wants to admit it. Everyone pretends their family is fine on social media while privately falling apart.

You need real support. People who get it.

Where to find support:

Other parents in the trenches: Find parents who are honest about struggles. Who can say "My teen is a nightmare right now" without judgment.

Parenting groups: Look for groups focused on positive parenting, collaborative approaches, or teenagers specifically.

Therapy: Individual therapy gives you a space to process your own stuff without burdening friends or family.

Partners: If you have a co-parent or partner, make sure you're supporting each other. Check in regularly about how you're both doing.

Friends without kids: They can remind you that you're a whole person beyond parenting. They give you space to be yourself.

Online communities: When in-person support isn't available, online groups can help. Just be selective. Avoid spaces that are mostly complaining without solutions.

Marcus found a parenting group specifically for parents of teens. Once a month, eight parents met for two hours. They shared struggles, gave each other advice, and provided perspective.

Just knowing he wasn't alone in finding parenting hard made an enormous difference. These parents got it. They weren't judging. They were surviving together.

What good support looks like:

- People who listen without trying to fix
- People who validate without enabling
- People who share their own struggles
- People who celebrate wins with you
- People who remind you of your strengths when you forget

If your current circle isn't providing this, actively seek out people who will.

20.5 The Marathon Mindset

Parenting teenagers is a marathon, not a sprint. You need to pace yourself.

Sprint mentality: Push through. Try harder. Don't show weakness. Power through exhaustion. Success means never struggling.

This leads to burnout.

Marathon mentality: Sustainable pace. Rest when needed. Celebrate progress. Accept that some days are hard. Success means staying in the race.

This is sustainable.

What marathon mindset looks like:

You prioritize your wellbeing: Sleep, exercise, nutrition, stress management. Not because you're selfish, but because you can't parent well if you're depleted.

You take breaks: You need time away from parenting. Alone time, friend time, hobby time. This isn't optional. It's necessary.

You accept imperfection: Some days you'll yell. Some days you'll fall back on old patterns. That's normal. Progress over perfection.

You adjust expectations: You can't be everything to everyone. Something has to give. Figure out what matters most and let other things go.

You celebrate small wins: Every good conversation counts. Every time you stay calm counts. Every day you show up counts. Notice and acknowledge your efforts.

You ask for help: You don't have to do this alone. Ask for help from partners, family, friends, professionals. Asking for help is strength, not weakness.

Jennifer realized she was running on empty. She worked full-time, parented alone, managed the household, and tried to be perfect at all of it. She was exhausted and resentful.

She made changes:

- Hired a cleaning service twice a month (worth every penny for her sanity)
- Started saying no to non-essential obligations
- Scheduled one night per week where she did something just for herself
- Went to therapy to process her stress
- Lowered her standards for cooking (frozen pizza is fine sometimes)
- Started exercising again (even just walks, but consistently)

These changes didn't solve everything. But she had more energy for the parenting challenges. She could stay calmer because she wasn't constantly depleted.

20.6 Celebrating Your Progress

You're probably focused on your teen's progress (or lack thereof). But your progress matters too.

Think about where you were when you started this book compared to now. What's different?

Maybe you:

- Stay calm more often
- Ask more questions instead of lecturing
- Listen better
- React less
- Reflect more
- Roll with resistance instead of fighting it
- See your teen's perspective more clearly
- Connect more deeply
- Trust the process

These are huge wins. Notice and celebrate them.

Ways to celebrate:

Acknowledge yourself: When you handle a situation well, mentally acknowledge it. "I stayed calm. That was hard. I did it."

Journal wins: Keep a log of parenting wins. On hard days, read back through it to remember you're making progress.

Share with support people: Tell your partner, friend, or therapist about conversations that went well. Let them celebrate with you.

Compare to past you: Not to other parents. To yourself six months ago. That's the only comparison that matters.

Appreciate relationship changes: If your connection with your teen has improved even slightly, that's worth celebrating.

Diego kept a note on his phone where he recorded good moments. "Stayed calm when Miguel lied about where he was." "Had a real conversation about college stress." "Miguel asked my advice about a friend situation."

On hard days, he'd read through the list and remember he was making progress, even when it didn't feel like it.

20.7 Final Reflections

You've reached the end of this book. But you're just at the beginning of a lifelong journey with your teen.

Parenting with MI is hard work. It requires self-awareness, emotional regulation, and consistent effort. You'll mess up. You'll lose your temper. You'll fall back into old patterns. That's part of being human.

What matters is the direction you're heading. Are you moving toward collaboration? Are you treating your teen with respect? Are you building a relationship that will last beyond their childhood?

If yes, you're doing it right.

Your teen might not appreciate this approach now. They might push back, test limits, and make your life difficult. That's normal. They're teenagers.

But years from now, they'll look back and recognize what you did. They'll appreciate that you respected them, listened to them, and treated them as capable people. They'll recreate this kind of relationship in their own lives.

And you'll have an adult child who wants to be in your life. Not out of obligation. Not because they have to. But because you built a relationship worth maintaining.

That's the gift of MI parenting.

Remember:

- You're enough
- You're doing better than you think
- Progress over perfection
- Your relationship with your teen is what matters most
- Take care of yourself
- Ask for help when you need it
- Celebrate small wins
- Keep showing up

You've got this. Not because you're perfect, but because you care enough to keep trying.

Thank you for reading this book. Thank you for showing up for your teen. Thank you for being willing to examine your approach and make changes.

Your teen is lucky to have you. Even if they don't say it.

Appendix A: Quick Reference MI Templates

You're in the middle of a difficult conversation with your teen. Your mind goes blank. What do you say next? This appendix gives you 15 ready-to-use conversation templates for the most common parent-teen conflicts. Use them as starting points, not scripts. Adapt the language to match your style and your teen's personality.

A.1 Homework Refusal

Situation: Your teen hasn't done homework all week. They're avoiding, making excuses, or outright refusing.

Traditional Approach: "You need to do your homework right now. I'm tired of this. No phone until it's done."

MI Approach:

Parent: "I noticed you haven't been doing homework this week. What's going on?"

Teen: "I don't know. I just don't feel like it."

Parent: "You're not feeling motivated right now." (Reflection)

Teen: "It's so boring and pointless."

Parent: "The work feels meaningless to you. Help me understand. What specifically feels pointless?" (Reflection plus open question)

Teen: "Like, why do I need to know about the Civil War? I'm never going to use that."

Parent: "You don't see how history connects to your life. What are you interested in?" (Reflection plus open question)

Teen: "I don't know. Music, I guess."

Parent: "Music matters to you. What's your plan for after high school?" (Affirmation plus open question)

Teen: "Maybe music production or sound engineering."

Parent: "That's a solid career path. What do you need to do to make that happen?" (Affirmation plus open question)

Teen: "I'd probably need to go to college. Or at least finish high school."

Parent: "So finishing high school, including passing history, connects to your music goals. What would help you get through the boring stuff?" (Developing discrepancy plus open question)

Teen: "I don't know. Maybe if I did homework right after school before I lose motivation?"

Parent: "That's a concrete plan. Want to try that this week and see how it goes?" (Affirmation plus invitation)

A.2 Coming Home Past Curfew

Situation: Your teen came home an hour late without calling or texting. You're worried and angry.

Traditional Approach: "Where were you? You're grounded for a month. I can't trust you anymore."

MI Approach:

Parent: "You came in at midnight. We agreed on 11. I was really worried. Tell me what happened." (Stating facts plus expressing concern plus open question)

Teen: "Sorry. We lost track of time."

Parent: "You weren't keeping track of the time. What were you doing?" (Reflection plus open question)

Teen: "Just hanging out at Maya's house."

Parent: "At Maya's house. Why didn't you text when you realized you'd be late?" (Reflection plus open question)

Teen: "I don't know. I figured you'd say no if I asked."

Parent: "You thought I'd make you come home, so you didn't ask. Here's my concern. When you don't come home and don't call, I don't know if you're safe. My mind goes to car accidents, bad situations, all the worst things." (Reflection plus honest sharing)

Teen: "I didn't think about it like that."

Parent: "I get that. In the moment, you're with friends having fun. But from my side, I'm responsible for making sure you're okay. How can we handle this differently next time?" (Empathy plus open question)

Teen: "I could text if I'm going to be late?"

Parent: "That would help a lot. And if you text before curfew asking for more time, I'm more likely to say yes than if you just don't show up. Can you do that?" (Affirmation plus clarification)

Teen: "Yeah, I can do that."

Parent: "Good. Now, there needs to be a consequence for tonight since we had an agreement and you broke it. What do you think is fair?" (Setting boundary plus inviting input)

A.3 Caught Lying

Situation: You discovered your teen lied about where they were going. Trust feels broken.

Traditional Approach: "I can't believe you lied to me! How am I supposed to trust you now?"

MI Approach:

Parent: "I need to talk to you about something serious. You told me you were at the library, but I saw on Find My Friends that you were at the mall. That's lying. I'm really disappointed." (Direct statement of facts and feelings)

Teen: "I knew you'd say no if I asked to go to the mall."

Parent: "You didn't think I'd give permission, so you lied instead." (Reflection)

Teen: "Yeah."

Parent: "I get that it feels easier in the moment to lie than to deal with me saying no. And it's also really damaging to our relationship. When you lie, I can't trust what you tell me. That makes me want to restrict your freedom more, not less." (Empathy plus consequence explanation)

Teen: "I'm sorry."

Parent: "I appreciate that. Help me understand. What is it about asking permission that feels so hard?" (Open question)

Teen: "You always say no to everything."

Parent: "It feels like I never let you do what you want. Is that actually true, or does it just feel that way?" (Reflection plus reality check)

Teen: (pause) "I guess you say yes sometimes. But I never know what you'll say."

Parent: "So it's unpredictable. That's frustrating. Here's what I'm thinking. I'd rather you ask and I say no than you lie. If you lie and I find out, the answer is always no in the future. If you ask honestly and I say no, we can talk about it. Maybe there's a compromise. Maybe I have a good reason. Maybe you can change my mind. But lying takes away all those options." (Reflection plus explanation of options)

Teen: "Okay. I get it."

Parent: "What would you need from me to feel like you can ask honestly?" (Open question)

Teen: "I don't know. Maybe if you'd actually listen instead of just automatically saying no?"

Parent: "You want me to really hear you out before deciding. That's fair. I can do that. And I need you to tell me the truth, even when it's hard. Deal?" (Reflection plus collaborative agreement)

A.4 Request for More Freedom

Situation: Your teen wants to stay out later, go somewhere unsupervised, or have more independence than you think they're ready for.

Traditional Approach: "No, you're too young for that. End of discussion."

MI Approach:

Parent: "Tell me about this party you want to go to." (Open question)

Teen: "It's at Jordan's house. Everyone's going. It's not a big deal."

Parent: "Everyone's going and it feels like a normal party. What time does it start and end?" (Reflection plus clarification)

Teen: "It starts at 8. I don't know when it ends."

Parent: "No set end time. Will Jordan's parents be there?" (Clarification)

Teen: "I think so. Maybe."

Parent: "You're not sure. I'm guessing there will be alcohol there?" (Clarification plus direct question)

Teen: "Probably. I'm not going to drink."

Parent: "You're planning to stay sober. I appreciate that. Here's my concern. A party with no clear end time, maybe no parents, and alcohol is a situation where things can go wrong fast. Not necessarily because of your choices, but because of others' choices. What's your plan if things get out of hand?" (Affirmation plus concern plus open question)

Teen: "I'd leave."

Parent: "You'd remove yourself from the situation. How would you get home?" (Reflection plus clarification)

Teen: "I could call you?"

Parent: "Yes, absolutely. Always. Any time, no questions asked, I'll come get you. Now, I'm thinking about whether this party is a good idea. What would make it safer?" (Affirmation plus open question)

Teen: "I don't know. If Jordan's parents were definitely there?"

Parent: "That would help. Here's what I'm willing to do. You confirm with Jordan that parents will be home the whole time. You go, but you check in with me every hour via text. I pick you up at 11. If things feel sketchy at any point, you call and I come immediately, no judgment. How does that sound?" (Collaborative solution)

Teen: "Okay, I guess that works."

A.5 Breaking House Rules

Situation: Your teen keeps breaking a household rule despite repeated reminders and consequences.

Traditional Approach: "I've told you a hundred times to clean up after yourself! I'm done reminding you!"

MI Approach:

Parent: "We need to talk about the kitchen. I've asked you multiple times to clean up after yourself when you make food. It's not happening. What's going on?" (Direct statement plus open question)

Teen: "I forget."

Parent: "You forget. Every time?" (Reflection plus gentle challenge)

Teen: "I mean, sometimes I just don't feel like it."

Parent: "Sometimes you don't feel motivated to clean up. I get that. Nobody loves cleaning. Here's the thing. We all live here. When you leave a mess, someone else has to clean it. Usually me. How is that fair?" (Reflection plus empathy plus open question)

Teen: "It's not, I guess."

Parent: "It's not. And I'm tired of nagging you about it. I'm guessing you're tired of being nagged. So we need a different solution. What ideas do you have?" (Validation plus open question)

Teen: "I don't know. I could try to remember better?"

Parent: "That hasn't worked so far. What would actually help you remember?" (Gentle reality check plus open question)

Teen: "Maybe a sign on the fridge?"

Parent: "That might help. What else?" (Encouraging more ideas)

Teen: "I could just do it right away before I sit down?"

Parent: "Clean up immediately instead of planning to do it later. That could work. Want to try that for a week?" (Reflection plus invitation)

Teen: "Sure."

Parent: "Okay. And if it's still not happening, we need to talk about logical consequences. If you're using the kitchen but not cleaning up, maybe you lose kitchen privileges for a bit until you can show you'll follow through. Does that seem fair?" (Clear consequence tied to behavior)

A.6 Friend Concerns

Situation: You're worried about your teen's friend group. You think they're a bad influence.

Traditional Approach: "I don't want you hanging out with those kids anymore. They're trouble."

MI Approach:

Parent: "I want to talk to you about your friends. I've noticed you've been spending a lot of time with a new group. Tell me about them." (Open question)

Teen: "They're just my friends. They're cool."

Parent: "You like them. What do you like about them?" (Reflection plus open question)

Teen: "They're fun. We just hang out and laugh and stuff."

Parent: "They're fun to be around. What kinds of things do you do together?" (Reflection plus open question)

Teen: "I don't know. Normal stuff. Go to the mall, play video games, whatever."

Parent: "Hanging out doing regular things. Can I share something I've noticed?" (Asking permission)

Teen: "I guess."

Parent: "I've noticed that since you started hanging out with this group, your grades have dropped and you seem more stressed. I'm wondering if there's a connection." (Observation without blame)

Teen: "I don't think so."

Parent: "Maybe not. Help me understand what's going on with school then." (Accepting their perspective plus open question)

Teen: "I don't know. School is just harder this year."

Parent: "It's more challenging. Are you getting enough time to study?" (Reflection plus open question)

Teen: "Not really. I'm always doing stuff with my friends."

Parent: "Time with friends is taking up study time. How do you feel about your grades right now?" (Reflection plus open question)

Teen: "Not great, honestly."

Parent: "They bother you. What's important to you about grades?" (Reflection plus values exploration)

Teen: "I need good grades to get into college."

Parent: "College matters to you. How do your current grades fit with that goal?" (Reflection plus developing discrepancy)

Teen: "They don't. I need to do better."

Parent: "So you're recognizing there's a gap. What would help?" (Reflection plus open question)

Teen: "I need to spend less time hanging out and more time studying."

Parent: "That sounds like a plan. I'm not saying stop seeing your friends. I'm saying find a balance that works. How could you do that?" (Clarifying plus open question)

A.7 School Problems

Situation: Your teen is struggling academically, behaviorally, or socially at school.

Traditional Approach: "You need to get your act together at school. I'm going to start checking your grades every day."

MI Approach:

Parent: "Your teacher called today. She said you're not turning in work and you've been disruptive in class. Talk to me about what's happening at school." (Stating facts plus open question)

Teen: "I hate that class. It's so boring."

Parent: "The class doesn't engage you. What makes it boring?" (Reflection plus open question)

Teen: "She just talks the whole time. I can't focus."

Parent: "It's hard to stay focused when it's all lecture. What helps you focus better?" (Reflection plus open question)

Teen: "I don't know. Hands-on stuff, I guess."

Parent: "You learn better by doing. This class doesn't match your learning style. That's frustrating. And you still have to pass it. What's your plan?" (Reflection plus empathy plus open question)

Teen: "I don't know."

Parent: "Let's think about this together. What grade are you hoping for in this class?" (Collaborative problem-solving)

Teen: "At least a C."

Parent: "Okay, a C. What would it take to get a C?" (Clarification)

Teen: "I'd have to turn in all the missing work and do okay on tests."

Parent: "Those are the concrete steps. What's getting in the way of turning in work?" (Reflection plus open question)

Teen: "I just don't care about it."

Parent: "You don't care about the subject. I get that. Do you care about passing?" (Reflection plus clarification)

Teen: "Yeah, I don't want to fail."

Parent: "You don't want to fail. So even though the subject is boring, the outcome matters. What support would help you get through this class?" (Reflection of value plus open question)

Teen: "Maybe a tutor? Or if you helped me understand the assignments?"

Parent: "Those are both options. Let's set up some support. And we need to talk about the behavior piece. Your teacher said you're being disruptive. What's that about?" (Agreeing to help plus addressing behavior)

A.8 Technology Battles

Situation: Screen time is constant. You've tried limits, parental controls, taking devices away. Nothing works.

Traditional Approach: "That's it! I'm taking your phone for a week. You're addicted."

MI Approach:

Parent: "I want to talk about phone use. I've noticed you're on your phone constantly from the moment you wake up until you go to sleep. What's that like for you?" (Observation plus open question)

Teen: "What do you mean?"

Parent: "How do you feel about how much you're on your phone?" (Clarification)

Teen: "I don't know. Everyone's on their phone all the time."

Parent: "It's normal in your world. And I'm curious how it affects you. Do you like being on it this much?" (Reflection plus open question)

Teen: "Sometimes it's fun. Sometimes I'm just doing it because there's nothing else to do."

Parent: "So sometimes you're enjoying it, sometimes it's just a habit. What do you notice about yourself when you're on your phone a lot versus when you're not?" (Reflection plus open question)

Teen: "I guess I'm more tired when I'm on it a lot. And I don't sleep as well."

Parent: "You've noticed effects on your energy and sleep. What else?" (Reflection plus invitation to elaborate)

Teen: "I feel kind of like I'm wasting time. Like, I'll scroll for an hour and then I don't even remember what I was looking at."

Parent: "That empty feeling after scrolling. Like the time disappeared but you didn't get anything from it." (Reflection)

Teen: "Yeah, exactly."

Parent: "So there are some real costs to being on your phone so much. What would be different if you used it less?" (Developing discrepancy)

Teen: "I'd probably sleep better. And maybe have more time for other stuff."

Parent: "Better sleep and time for other activities. What other stuff would you want to do?" (Reflection plus open question)

Teen: "I used to draw. I haven't done that in forever."

Parent: "You miss drawing. Your phone time is taking up space that used to be for creativity." (Reflection of values)

Teen: "I guess, yeah."

Parent: "What would a healthier relationship with your phone look like?" (Open question)

Teen: "Maybe limit it to like an hour or two a day? And not first thing in the morning or right before bed."

Parent: "Specific time limits and no phones around sleep. Those are concrete ideas. How would you make that actually happen?" (Reflection plus open question)

A.9 Substance Use Discovery

Situation: You found evidence of marijuana, vaping, or alcohol use. You're scared and angry.

Traditional Approach: "How could you be so stupid? You're grounded indefinitely. I'm going to drug test you every week."

MI Approach:

Parent: "I found a vape pen in your backpack. I need you to be honest with me. Are you vaping?" (Direct, calm statement)

Teen: "It's not mine. I'm holding it for a friend."

Parent: "Is that true?" (Direct question)

Teen: (pause) "No. It's mine."

Parent: "Thank you for being honest. That takes courage. How long have you been vaping?" (Affirmation plus open question)

Teen: "A few months."

Parent: "A few months. Tell me about it. Why did you start?" (Reflection plus open question)

Teen: "Everyone does it. It's not a big deal."

Parent: "It's normal in your friend group and you don't see it as harmful. I hear that. Can I share what I know about vaping?" (Reflection plus asking permission)

Teen: "Sure."

Parent: "Vaping nicotine is highly addictive, especially for teenage brains that are still developing. Most people who start think they can quit anytime, but nicotine changes your brain chemistry. It's hard to stop once you've started. I'm not trying to scare you, I'm telling you facts. Does that match what you've noticed?" (Education plus open question)

Teen: "I mean, I do think about it a lot. Like, I want to vape all the time."

Parent: "You're noticing the addictive pull. That's important to recognize. What concerns you about vaping?" (Reflection plus open question)

Teen: "I don't know. I guess I don't want to be addicted to something."

Parent: "Independence matters to you. Not being controlled by a substance." (Reflection of value)

Teen: "Yeah."

Parent: "What are you thinking about all this?" (Open question)

Teen: "I don't know. Maybe I should quit."

Parent: "You're considering quitting. What would help you do that?" (Reflection plus open question)

Teen: "I'd need to tell my friends I'm not vaping anymore. And get rid of my vape pen."

Parent: "Those are concrete first steps. How can I support you?" (Reflection plus offer of support)

Teen: "Just don't freak out if I struggle with it."

Parent: "I won't freak out. I want you to be honest with me about how it's going. If you slip up, we talk about it and figure out what to do differently. We're in this together. But I need to be clear, there will be consequences for lying or hiding use. Honesty keeps us connected." (Reassurance plus clear boundary)

A.10 Disrespectful Behavior

Situation: Your teen is being rude, talking back, rolling eyes, or being outright disrespectful.

Traditional Approach: "Don't you dare talk to me that way! Go to your room and don't come out until you can be respectful!"

MI Approach:

Parent: "Hey. We need to pause. The way you're talking to me right now is disrespectful. I'm not okay with it." (Clear boundary)

Teen: (rolls eyes, doesn't respond)

Parent: "I see you rolling your eyes. You're frustrated with me. What's going on?" (Observation plus open question)

Teen: "You're being ridiculous."

Parent: "You think I'm being unreasonable. Tell me your side." (Reflection plus invitation)

Teen: "You won't let me do anything!"

Parent: "It feels like I'm too controlling and you don't have freedom. That's really frustrating. And the way you're expressing it, with eye rolling and calling me ridiculous, is disrespectful. I want to hear what you're upset about, but I need you to talk to me with basic courtesy." (Reflection plus empathy plus boundary)

Teen: "Fine."

Parent: "Thank you. Now tell me what's actually bothering you." (Acknowledgment plus open question)

Teen: "I wanted to go to the movies with friends and you said no for no reason."

Parent: "I said no and you don't understand why. Let me explain my thinking. You have a test tomorrow that you haven't studied for. My concern is that if you go to the movies tonight, you won't study and you'll do poorly. Does that make sense even if you don't like it?" (Reflection plus explanation)

Teen: "I guess."

Parent: "I'm not trying to control you or ruin your fun. I'm trying to help you make choices that set you up for success. And we can disagree about decisions. But we talk about it respectfully. When you're disrespectful, I shut down and so does the conversation. Make sense?" (Clarifying intention plus explaining consequence)

Teen: "Yeah. Sorry."

Parent: "I appreciate the apology. Now, let's talk about the movies. What if you study for two hours tonight, and if you get that done, you can go to a later showing?" (Affirmation plus collaborative solution)

A.11 Room Cleanliness

Situation: Your teen's room is a disaster. You've asked them to clean it repeatedly. Nothing changes.

Traditional Approach: "Your room is disgusting! Clean it right now or I'm throwing everything on the floor in the trash!"

MI Approach:

Parent: "We need to talk about your room. It's gotten pretty bad in there. What's going on?" (Observation plus open question)

Teen: "It's my room. Why do you care?"

Parent: "You're right that it's your space. I care because old food attracts bugs, dirty clothes start to smell, and I'm concerned about hygiene. Plus, can you even find things in there?" (Acknowledging autonomy plus explaining concerns plus practical question)

Teen: "I can find stuff."

Parent: "You know where things are. What about the smell and the old food?" (Accepting their answer plus returning to concern)

Teen: "I'll clean it eventually."

Parent: "Eventually. When?" (Gentle challenge)

Teen: "I don't know. When I feel like it."

Parent: "When you feel motivated. Here's the thing. That motivation hasn't come in three months. So I'm wondering what would help you feel motivated." (Reflection plus open question)

Teen: "I don't know. Cleaning is boring."

Parent: "It's boring. Everyone feels that way. And it still needs to happen. What would make it less painful?" (Empathy plus open question)

Teen: "Maybe if you helped?"

Parent: "I could help for 30 minutes if you're willing to work on it for 30 minutes. But I'm not doing it for you. It's your room, so you're responsible for maintaining it. Sound fair?" (Conditional offer)

Teen: "I guess."

Parent: "Okay. And going forward, I need you to keep it to a basic standard. Trash out, no food left out, and dirty clothes in the hamper. Not perfect, just livable. Can you do that?" (Setting clear minimum standard)

Teen: "Yeah, probably."

Parent: "Let's try it. And if it gets bad again, we talk about what's getting in the way." (Agreement plus follow-up plan)

A.12 Sibling Conflicts

Situation: Your teens are constantly fighting. You're tired of being referee.

Traditional Approach: "I don't care who started it! Both of you go to your rooms right now!"

MI Approach:

Parent: "Okay, everyone stop. I'm not going to referee another fight. We're going to talk about this differently. Marcus, what happened from your perspective?" (Setting boundary plus open question)

Marcus: "He took my charger without asking."

Parent: "He took your charger. Javier, what happened from your side?" (Reflection plus open question to other)

Javier: "I just borrowed it for five minutes. He's being dramatic."

Parent: "You needed it briefly and don't think it's a big deal. Marcus, what bothers you about that?" (Reflection plus open question)

Marcus: "He's always taking my stuff. Every single day."

Parent: "It's not about the charger. It's about a pattern of him taking things without permission. That feels disrespectful." (Reflection of underlying issue)

Marcus: "Exactly!"

Parent: "Javier, did you know it bothered him this much?" (Open question)

Javier: "I guess. But it's just a charger."

Parent: "To you it's not a big deal. To him, it's about respecting boundaries. How would you feel if he constantly took your stuff?" (Perspective-taking)

Javier: "I'd be annoyed."

Parent: "Right. So here's what I'm thinking. You two need to figure out how to live together without constant conflict. I'm not going to solve every fight. What would help you get along better?" (Putting responsibility on them plus open question)

Marcus: "He could ask before taking my stuff."

Parent: "Asking permission. Javier, can you do that?" (Clarification)

Javier: "Fine."

Parent: "And Marcus, when he asks, will you let him borrow things sometimes?" (Reciprocal expectation)

Marcus: "If he asks and brings it back, yeah."

Parent: "Good. You just solved it yourselves. That's what I want to see more of. Figure it out between you before bringing me into it." (Affirmation plus expectation)

A.13 Money and Spending

Situation: Your teen spent all their money and now wants you to buy them something.

Traditional Approach: "No! You should have thought about that before you wasted your money. This is your problem."

MI Approach:

Parent: "You're asking me to buy you these shoes. You have money. Why aren't you using it?" (Clarifying question)

Teen: "I spent it."

Parent: "On what?" (Open question)

Teen: "Just stuff. Eating out with friends, mostly."

Parent: "Going out to eat. How much money do you have left?" (Reflection plus clarification)

Teen: "Like $5."

Parent: "So you spent $95 in two weeks on eating out, and now you need shoes. I'm not going to buy them for you. This is a natural consequence of spending all your money." (Stating consequence)

Teen: "But I need shoes for gym!"

Parent: "You do need shoes. How can you get them?" (Agreeing plus open question)

Teen: "I don't know. Can't you just buy them?"

Parent: "I could. And I'm not going to. You had the money and chose to spend it on other things. What are your options now?" (Staying firm plus open question)

Teen: "I guess I have to wait until I get more money."

Parent: "That's one option. Any others?" (Affirming plus pushing for more)

Teen: "I could do extra chores to earn money faster?"

Parent: "You could. Or borrow from next month's allowance and pay it back. You have choices. What do you want to do?" (Offering options plus autonomy)

Teen: "Can I do extra chores?"

Parent: "Yes. Let's figure out what chores and how much they're worth. And I want you to think about what you learned from this. You wanted shoes and eating out. You chose eating out. Now you don't have shoes. Next time, how will you handle money differently?" (Practical solution plus reflection prompt)

Teen: "I need to think about what I really want before I spend money on random stuff."

Parent: "Exactly. You just learned something about budgeting the hard way." (Affirmation)

A.14 Dating Concerns

Situation: Your teen is dating someone and you have concerns about the relationship.

Traditional Approach: "I don't like this person. I don't want you seeing them anymore."

MI Approach:

Parent: "You've been dating Riley for a few months now. Tell me about the relationship. How's it going?" (Open question)

Teen: "It's good. I really like them."

Parent: "You're happy. What do you like about Riley?" (Reflection plus open question)

Teen: "They're fun and nice to me."

Parent: "They treat you well. That's important. Can I share something I've noticed?" (Affirmation plus asking permission)

Teen: "I guess."

Parent: "I've noticed that since you started dating Riley, you don't see your other friends as much. You used to hang out with Maya and Jordan all the time. What's going on with that?" (Observation plus open question)

Teen: "I don't know. Riley doesn't really like my friends."

Parent: "Riley doesn't like your friends, so you stopped seeing them. How do you feel about that?" (Reflection plus open question)

Teen: "I mean, it's fine. Riley is more important."

Parent: "Your relationship with Riley matters most right now. And I'm wondering what happens to you when all your time and energy goes to one person. Do you ever feel like you're losing yourself?" (Reflection plus open question)

Teen: "Sometimes, maybe."

Parent: "Sometimes you do. What's that like?" (Reflection plus elaboration)

Teen: "I don't know. Sometimes I feel like I can't do anything without checking with Riley first."

Parent: "That sounds exhausting. Like you're not free to make your own choices. Is that how you want a relationship to feel?" (Empathy plus open question)

Teen: "No, I guess not."

Parent: "What would a healthy relationship look like to you?" (Values exploration)

Teen: "I don't know. Maybe where I still have my own friends and hobbies and stuff?"

Parent: "Where you have your own life and also a relationship. Both things, not one or the other. Does your current relationship match that?" (Reflection plus discrepancy)

Teen: "Not really."

Parent: "What would you want to change?" (Open question)

Teen: "Maybe I should talk to Riley about seeing my friends more?"

Parent: "That's a start. And if Riley isn't okay with that, what does that tell you?" (Affirmation plus critical thinking)

A.15 College and Future Planning

Situation: Your teen has no plan for after high school and it's stressing you out.

Traditional Approach: "You need to figure out what you're doing with your life. You can't just sit around after graduation."

MI Approach:

Parent: "You're a junior now. Have you thought about what you want to do after high school?" (Open question)

Teen: "Not really."

Parent: "You haven't thought about it much. What's your general sense? College, work, gap year, military, trade school?" (Reflection plus offering options)

Teen: "I don't know. Maybe college?"

Parent: "College is a possibility. What makes you think about college?" (Open question)

Teen: "I don't know. That's just what people do."

Parent: "It's the expected path. And it's also expensive and a big commitment. I want you to choose it because it's right for you, not because it's expected. What interests you?" (Reflection plus open question)

Teen: "I like working with computers."

Parent: "Computers interest you. What about them?" (Reflection plus open question)

Teen: "I don't know. Building them, coding, gaming. All of it."

Parent: "So technology in general. That's a growing field with lots of paths. Have you looked into careers in tech?" (Reflection plus exploration)

Teen: "Not really."

Parent: "Want to explore that together? We could look at what education you'd need for different tech careers. Some might need a four-year degree. Some might need a two-year degree or certification. Some you could learn through bootcamps. There are options." (Offering to explore without pressure)

Teen: "That would be helpful."

Parent: "Good. Let's do that. And here's what I want you thinking about. What kind of life do you want as an adult? Where do you want to live? What matters to you about work? Do you want to make a lot of money, or does job satisfaction matter more? These questions help guide decisions." (Values exploration)

Teen: "I want to make enough money to live comfortably. And I want to not hate my job."

Parent: "Comfortable income and job satisfaction. Those are good goals. As we look at options, we'll keep those in mind. And you don't have to have it all figured out right now. But you do need to start thinking about it. Sound fair?" (Reflection plus reasonable expectation)

Teen: "Yeah, that's fair."

A.16 Using These Templates

These templates are starting points, not scripts. Your conversations will go differently based on your teen's personality, your relationship, and the specific situation. The patterns remain the same: ask open questions, reflect what you hear, develop discrepancy between behavior and values, and collaborate on solutions.

The more you practice, the more natural it becomes. You'll stop needing templates because the MI approach will become your default way of communicating.

Appendix B: MI Cheat Sheets

Need a quick reminder of MI skills in the middle of a conversation? These cheat sheets give you fast reference guides to the core MI techniques. Keep them handy until the approach becomes second nature.

B.1 OARS at a Glance

Open Questions

- Start with what, how, or tell me about
- Can't be answered with yes/no
- Invite thinking and reflection
- Give your teen space to talk

Examples:

- "What's going on?"
- "How do you feel about that?"
- "Tell me more."
- "What are you thinking?"
- "Help me understand."

Affirmations

- Notice strengths and efforts
- Recognize positive qualities
- Acknowledge difficulty
- Build confidence
- Focus on process, not just outcomes

Examples:

- "You're handling this with maturity."
- "I see how hard you're working on this."
- "That took courage to admit."
- "You're thinking this through carefully."
- "I appreciate your honesty."

Reflections

- Say back what you heard
- Show understanding
- Don't add, don't judge
- Let them hear themselves
- Keep it simple

Examples:

- "You're feeling overwhelmed."
- "This situation is frustrating."
- "You're not sure what to do."
- "That hurt your feelings."
- "You're worried about the outcome."

Summaries

- Pull together multiple points
- Show the big picture
- Capture both sides of ambivalence
- Invite correction
- Transition to next topic

Examples:

- "So you're saying you want more freedom, and you also recognize you haven't been as responsible lately. Does that sound right?"
- "Let me make sure I understand. You're stressed about school, your friends are pressuring you, and you're not sleeping well. Anything else?"

B.2 Change Talk Recognition

Desire: Wanting change

- "I want to..."
- "I wish I could..."
- "I'd like to..."
- "It would be nice if..."

Ability: Seeing capability

- "I can..."

- "I could..."
- "I'm able to..."
- "It's possible for me to..."

Reasons: Benefits of change

- "It would help me..."
- "I'd feel better if..."
- "That would make things easier..."
- "It would be worth it because..."

Need: Urgency for change

- "I need to..."
- "I have to..."
- "I've got to..."
- "It's necessary to..."

Commitment: Pledging action

- "I will..."
- "I'm going to..."
- "I promise..."
- "I'll definitely..."

Activation: Readiness to act

- "I'm ready to..."
- "I'm prepared to..."
- "I'm willing to..."

Taking Steps: Already acting

- "I've started..."
- "I already..."
- "Yesterday I..."
- "I've been..."

When you hear change talk, strengthen it with reflections and follow-up questions.

B.3 Common MI Mistakes

Asking "why" questions

- Sounds accusatory
- Puts people on defensive
- Instead: "What led to that?" or "Help me understand."

Reflecting with question marks

- "You're feeling sad?"
- Sounds uncertain or doubting
- Instead: "You're feeling sad." (statement)

Multiple questions at once

- "What happened and how did you feel and what did you do?"
- Overwhelming and confusing
- Instead: One question at a time

Premature problem-solving

- Jumping to solutions before understanding
- Skipping the exploration phase
- Instead: Stay curious longer

Fake reflections

- "So what you're saying is you're being irresponsible."
- Adding judgment to reflection
- Instead: Neutral, non-judgmental reflection

The righting reflex

- Immediate urge to fix and advise
- Takes over collaboration
- Instead: Trust the process, ask more questions

Interrogation

- Question after question without reflection
- Feels like an interview
- Instead: Balance questions with reflections

Agreeing with sustain talk

- "You're right, change is too hard."
- Reinforces resistance
- Instead: Reflect neutrally, then pivot to change talk

Over-doing OARS

- Sounds robotic and unnatural
- Makes teen suspicious
- Instead: Use techniques selectively and naturally

B.4 Questions That Elicit Change Talk

For Desire:

- "What would you like to be different?"
- "If things could be exactly how you wanted, what would that look like?"
- "What do you wish would change?"

For Ability:

- "What makes you think you could do this if you decided to?"
- "How might you go about making this change?"
- "What gives you confidence you could succeed?"

For Reasons:

- "What would be the benefits of changing?"
- "How would things be better if you made this change?"
- "What would this do for you?"

For Need:

- "How important is this to you?"
- "What would have to happen for this to be a priority?"
- "How urgent does this feel?"

For Commitment:

- "What are you going to do?"
- "What's your plan?"

- "What's the next step?"

For values connection:

- "What matters most to you?"
- "How does this fit with what's important to you?"
- "What kind of person do you want to be?"

For discrepancy:

- "How does this behavior fit with your goals?"
- "What concerns you about continuing as you are?"
- "On the one hand... on the other hand... how do you make sense of that?"

For elaboration:

- "Tell me more about that."
- "What else?"
- "In what ways?"
- "Can you give me an example?"

B.5 Reflective Listening Stems

Simple reflections:

- "You feel..."
- "You're thinking..."
- "It sounds like..."
- "You're saying..."
- "What I'm hearing is..."

Continuing the paragraph:

- "And you..."
- "So you..."
- "Which means..."

Amplified reflections (slight exaggeration to invite correction):

- "So you're never going to..."
- "You absolutely can't..."

- Use carefully and sparingly

Double-sided reflections (both sides of ambivalence):

- "On one hand you... and on the other hand you..."
- "Part of you wants... and part of you..."

Feeling reflections:

- "That must feel..."
- "It sounds frustrating..."
- "You seem worried..."

Meaning reflections:

- "This matters because..."
- "What you're really saying is..."
- "The deeper issue is..."

Metaphor reflections:

- "It's like..."
- "You're describing it as..."

Remember: End reflections with a period, not a question mark. State them confidently, even if you're not 100% sure. Your teen will correct you if you're wrong, which gives them a chance to clarify their thinking.

B.6 Values Exploration Questions

Use these questions to help your teen identify what matters most to them:

Big picture:

- "What's most important to you in life?"
- "What do you care about deeply?"
- "If you could be remembered for one thing, what would it be?"
- "What do you want your life to stand for?"

Relationships:

- "What kind of friend do you want to be?"

- "What matters to you in relationships?"
- "How do you want people to feel when they're around you?"

Character:

- "What qualities do you admire in others?"
- "What kind of person are you trying to become?"
- "What personal traits do you value most?"

Future:

- "Five years from now, what do you hope is true about your life?"
- "When you imagine your adult self, what do you see?"
- "What legacy do you want to leave?"

Current behavior:

- "How do your current choices reflect your values?"
- "Where is there a gap between what you value and how you're acting?"
- "If you were living according to your values, what would be different?"

Use these answers to develop discrepancy when behavior doesn't match stated values. The gap between values and actions creates motivation for change.

Appendix C: Worksheets and Tools

These practical worksheets and tools support the MI conversations you're having with your teen. You can recreate these on paper, or adapt them digitally. Use them to structure difficult conversations, track progress, and create clear agreements.

C.1 Importance and Confidence Rulers

Purpose: Quickly assess how important change feels to your teen and how confident they are in their ability to change.

How to use: Ask your teen to rate on a scale of 1 to 10.

Importance Ruler: "On a scale of 1 to 10, where 1 is not at all important and 10 is extremely important, how important is it to you to [make this change]?"

If they say 7:

- "Why a 7 and not a 2?" (This elicits reasons why it IS important)
- "What would make it an 8 or 9?" (This identifies what would increase importance)

Confidence Ruler: "On a scale of 1 to 10, where 1 is not at all confident and 10 is extremely confident, how confident are you that you could [make this change] if you decided to?"

If they say 4:

- "Why a 4 and not a 0?" (This elicits existing self-efficacy)
- "What would make it a 6 or 7?" (This identifies barriers to address)

Template:

Issue: _____

Importance (1-10): ____
Why this number and not lower? _____
What would raise it? _____

Confidence (1-10): ____
Why this number and not lower? _____
What would raise it? _____

C.2 Decisional Balance Worksheet

Purpose: Help your teen examine pros and cons of changing versus staying the same.

How to use: Fill in all four quadrants together. Let your teen do most of the talking. You just write and ask clarifying questions.

Template:

Behavior we're discussing: _____

BENEFITS of CHANGING | COSTS of CHANGING
(Why change is good) | (Why change is hard)
_____|_____
                     |
                     |
                     |
_____|_____

BENEFITS of STAYING SAME | COSTS of STAYING SAME
(Why not changing is easy) | (Why not changing is bad)
_____|_____
                     |
                     |
                     |

After completing:

- "What stands out to you looking at this?"
- "Which quadrant matters most?"
- "What does this tell you?"

The most motivating quadrants are usually BENEFITS of changing and COSTS of staying the same.

C.3 Values Clarification Exercise

Purpose: Help your teen identify their core values and assess how well current life aligns with those values.

Step 1: Brainstorm values Have your teen circle or highlight values that resonate from this list (or add their own):

Honesty, Creativity, Family, Friends, Independence, Learning, Health, Adventure, Helping Others, Success, Fun, Respect, Courage, Kindness, Fairness, Freedom, Loyalty, Achievement, Peace, Spirituality, Authenticity, Growth, Connection, Responsibility, Justice

Step 2: Choose top five From the values they identified, choose the five most important.

Step 3: Rate current alignment For each top value, rate 1 to 10 how much their current life reflects that value.

Template:

My Top 5 Values and Current Alignment:

1. _____ Current rating: ___/10
   What would move this higher? _____

2. _____ Current rating: ___/10
   What would move this higher? _____

3. _____ Current rating: ___/10
   What would move this higher? _____

4. _____ Current rating: ___/10
   What would move this higher? _____

5. _____ Current rating: ___/10
   What would move this higher? _____

Step 4: Connect to behavior "Looking at these gaps, what specific behavior would help close them?"

C.4 Communication Self Assessment

Purpose: Help you honestly assess your current communication patterns with your teen.

Rate yourself 1 to 10 on each item (1 = never, 10 = always):

_____ I listen more than I talk
_____ I ask questions instead of giving advice
_____ I stay calm when my teen is upset
_____ I validate feelings before problem-solving
_____ I avoid "why" questions that sound accusatory
_____ I reflect back what I hear without adding judgment

_____ I notice and affirm efforts and strengths
_____ I involve my teen in solving problems
_____ I express concerns without lecturing
_____ I respect my teen's perspective even when I disagree
_____ I avoid sarcasm and put-downs
_____ I apologize when I handle things badly
_____ I follow through on agreements
_____ I stay curious instead of judgmental
_____ I allow my teen to experience natural consequences

Total Score: _____ /150

Below 75: Significant room for improvement
75-105: Making progress, keep working at it
105-135: Solid communication, refine skills
135+: Strong collaborative communication

Use this to identify specific areas to focus on improving.

C.5 Weekly Practice Log

Purpose: Track your MI practice to build skills and notice progress.

How to use: Each time you use MI with your teen, briefly note what happened and what you learned.

Template:

Week of: _____

Day/Date: _____
Situation: _____
MI skills I used: _____
What went well: _____
What I'd do differently: _____

Day/Date: _____
Situation: _____
MI skills I used: _____
What went well: _____
What I'd do differently: _____

[Repeat for each day]

Weekly reflection:
What am I getting better at? _____
What do I need to work on? _____
What surprised me this week? _____

C.6 Teen Parent Agreement Template

Purpose: Create clear, collaborative agreements that both parties commit to.

Template:

Agreement Between: _____ and _____
Date: _____
Topic: _____

THE ISSUE:
What we're addressing: _____

WHAT TEEN AGREES TO DO:
1. _____
2. _____
3. _____

WHAT PARENT AGREES TO DO:
1. _____
2. _____
3. _____

HOW WE'LL KNOW IT'S WORKING:
_____

IF AGREEMENT ISN'T WORKING:
We will: _____

TRIAL PERIOD:
We'll try this for _____ weeks, then review on _____

Teen signature: _____ Date: _____
Parent signature: _____ Date: _____

REVIEW DATE:
What's working: _____
What needs adjustment: _____
Changes we're making: _____

C.7 Progress Tracking Sheet

Purpose: Track your teen's progress toward goals to celebrate wins and adjust when needed.

Template:

Teen's Name: _____

Goal: _____
Start Date: _____

Week 1: _____
Actions taken: _____
Successes: _____
Challenges: _____
Adjustments needed: _____

Week 2: _____
Actions taken: _____
Successes: _____
Challenges: _____
Adjustments needed: _____

[Repeat for each week]

Monthly Summary:
Overall progress: _____
What's working: _____
What needs to change: _____
Celebration: _____

Use these tools flexibly. Adapt them to fit your family. The goal is structure and clarity, not rigid adherence to forms.

Appendix D: Additional Resources

You've learned MI skills from this book. Now you want to go deeper, get support, or find help for specific challenges. This appendix points you to additional resources that can help.

D.1 Recommended Reading

On Motivational Interviewing: *Motivational Interviewing: Helping People Change* by William R. Miller and Stephen Rollnick. The definitive text on MI. More clinical than this book, but excellent for deeper understanding.

Motivational Interviewing with Adolescents and Young Adults by Sylvie Naar and Supriya Misra. Specifically focused on teens and young adults.

On Parenting Teens: *The Yes Brain* by Daniel Siegel and Tina Payne Bryson. Understanding teen brain development and responding effectively.

How to Talk So Teens Will Listen and Listen So Teens Will Talk by Adele Faber and Elaine Mazlish. Practical communication strategies.

The Teenage Brain by Frances E. Jensen. Neuroscience of adolescence explained for parents.

On Specific Challenges: *The Gift of Failure* by Jessica Lahey. Stepping back and letting teens learn from natural consequences.

Untangled: Guiding Teenage Girls Through the Seven Transitions into Adulthood by Lisa Damour. Specific to raising girls.

Raising Cain by Dan Kindlon and Michael Thompson. Specific to raising boys.

D.2 Online MI Training

Several organizations offer online training in MI specifically for parents:

Look for parent training through:

- Motivational Interviewing Network of Trainers (MINT)
- Center for Motivation and Change
- Local mental health organizations offering parent workshops

- Community colleges and adult education programs
- Online platforms offering parenting courses

Search terms to use: "Motivational Interviewing for Parents," "MI Parent Training," "Collaborative Parenting Workshops"

D.3 Support Groups and Forums

In-person support:

- Local parenting groups (check community centers, schools, churches)
- Parent support groups through school counselors
- Family therapy centers often offer parent groups
- Hospital systems sometimes offer parent education series

Online communities: Look for moderated forums focused on positive parenting approaches. Be selective. Avoid groups that are primarily venting without solutions.

D.4 Apps and Digital Tools

For tracking and organization (helpful for teens with executive function challenges):

- Google Calendar or similar for shared family schedules
- Todoist, Microsoft To Do, or similar for task management
- Screen time tracking apps built into phones
- Study timer apps (Pomodoro technique)

For mental health support:

- Crisis Text Line (text HOME to 741741)
- Calm, Headspace, or similar for meditation and anxiety
- Mood tracking apps if recommended by therapist

For family communication:

- Shared family organization apps
- Private family messaging groups
- Shared note-taking apps for agreements

D.5 Mental Health Resources

When to seek professional help:

- Persistent depression or anxiety
- Suicidal thoughts or self-harm
- Substance abuse beyond experimentation
- Eating disorders
- Trauma responses
- Severe behavioral problems
- Family conflict that's unmanageable

How to find help:

- Ask your teen's pediatrician for referrals
- Check with your insurance for covered providers
- School counselors can recommend local therapists
- Community mental health centers offer sliding-scale fees
- Online therapy platforms if local options limited

What to look for:

- Licensed therapist (LCSW, LMFT, LPC, psychologist)
- Experience with adolescents
- Approach that resonates with you and your teen
- Willingness to involve family when appropriate
- Cultural competence if relevant

D.6 Crisis Hotlines

Keep these numbers accessible:

National Suicide Prevention Lifeline: 988 24/7 support for people in suicidal crisis or emotional distress

Crisis Text Line: Text HOME to 741741 24/7 text support for people in crisis

SAMHSA National Helpline: 800-662-4357 Substance abuse and mental health information and referrals

National Domestic Violence Hotline: 800-799-7233 For teens experiencing dating violence

Trevor Project (LGBTQ+ youth): 866-488-7386 Crisis support for LGBTQ+ young people

Trans Lifeline: 877-565-8860 Support for transgender people

National Eating Disorders Association: 800-931-2237 Support and resources for eating disorders

D.7 Professional MI Training

If you're a professional who works with teens (therapist, counselor, teacher, coach, youth worker) and want formal MI training:

Motivational Interviewing Network of Trainers (MINT): The international organization for MI training. Their website lists trainers worldwide who offer workshops.

Training levels:

- Introductory workshops (2 days typically)
- Advanced training for skill refinement
- TNT (Training New Trainers) for those wanting to train others

What to expect:

- Didactic teaching of MI principles
- Lots of practice through role-plays
- Video examples and analysis
- Feedback on your MI skills
- Ongoing coaching recommended for skill development

MI is a skill that develops over time with practice and feedback. Reading this book is just the beginning. Real proficiency comes from consistent application and reflection on what works.

D.8 Final Encouragement

You've reached the end of this book. You have tools, templates, and resources. Now comes the hardest part: actually using what you've learned.

Start small. Pick one skill and focus on that this week. Maybe just asking more open questions. Next week, add reflective listening. Build gradually.

You'll mess up. You'll forget everything you learned and fall back into old patterns. That's normal. The goal isn't perfection. It's progress.

Your willingness to change your approach shows how much you love your teen. That matters more than getting every conversation right.

You're doing hard, important work. Be patient with yourself. Celebrate small wins. Ask for help when you need it.

Your teen is lucky to have a parent who cares this much.

References

- Ahrons, C. R. (2007). Family ties after divorce: Long-term implications for children. *Family Process, 46*(1), 53–65.
- Amrhein, P. C., Miller, W. R., Yahne, C. E., Palmer, M., & Fulcher, L. (2003). Client commitment language during motivational interviewing predicts drug use outcomes. *Journal of Consulting and Clinical Psychology, 71*(5), 862–878.
- Anderson, M., & Jiang, J. (2018, May 31). *Teens, social media & technology 2018*. Pew Research Center.
- Barkley, R. A. (Ed.). (2015). *Attention-deficit hyperactivity disorder: A handbook for diagnosis and treatment* (4th ed.). Guilford Press.
- Deci, E. L., & Ryan, R. M. (2000). The "what" and "why" of goal pursuits: Human needs and the self-determination of behavior. *Psychological Inquiry, 11*(4), 227–268.
- Greene, R. W. (2014). *The explosive child: A new approach for understanding and parenting easily frustrated, chronically inflexible children*. Harper.
- Grolnick, W. S. (2003). *The psychology of parental control: How well-meant parenting backfires*. Lawrence Erlbaum Associates.
- Harlow, J. W. (2024). _Motivational interviewing for beginners: A step-by-step guide to creating meaningful change_. Jstone Publishing.
- Hennessy, M., Bleakley, A., & Fishbein, M. (2010). Predicting intentions to use marijuana among adolescents: The effects of descriptive and injunctive social norms. *Journal of Youth and Adolescence, 39*(11), 1259–1268.
- Johnston, L. D., Miech, R. A., O'Malley, P. M., Bachman, J. G., Schulenberg, J. E., & Patrick, M. E. (2020). *Monitoring the Future national survey results on drug use 1975–2019*. Institute for Social Research, University of Michigan.
- Kazdin, A. E. (2008). *The Kazdin method for parenting the defiant child*. Houghton Mifflin.
- Miller, W. R., & Rollnick, S. (2013). *Motivational interviewing: Helping people change* (3rd ed.). Guilford Press.
- Moyers, T. B., & Miller, W. R. (2013). Is low therapist empathy toxic? *Psychology of Addictive Behaviors, 27*(3), 878–884.
- Naar, S., & Safren, S. A. (2017). *Motivational interviewing and CBT: Combining strategies for maximum effectiveness*. Guilford Press.
- Naar-King, S., & Suarez, M. (2011). *Motivational interviewing with adolescents and young adults*. Guilford Press.

- National Institute of Mental Health. (2024, September). *Mental illness.*
- Neff, K. D. (2003). Self-compassion: An alternative conceptualization of a healthy attitude toward oneself. *Self and Identity, 2*(2), 85–101.
- Patterson, G. R., & Forgatch, M. S. (1985). Therapist behavior as a determinant for client noncompliance: A paradox for the behavior modifier. *Journal of Consulting and Clinical Psychology, 53*(6), 846–851.
- Prochaska, J. O., & DiClemente, C. C. (1983). Stages and processes of self-change of smoking: Toward an integrative model of change. *Journal of Consulting and Clinical Psychology, 51*(3), 390–395.
- Prizant, B. M. (2015). *Uniquely human: A different way of seeing autism.* Simon & Schuster.
- Reid Chassiakos, Y. R., Radesky, J., Christakis, D., Moreno, M. A., Cross, C., & Council on Communications and Media. (2016). Children and adolescents and digital media. *Pediatrics, 138*(5), e20162593.
- Ryan, R. M., & Deci, E. L. (2000). Self-determination theory and the facilitation of intrinsic motivation, social development, and well-being. *American Psychologist, 55*(1), 68–78.
- Siegel, D. J., & Hartzell, M. (2003). *Parenting from the inside out: How a deeper self-understanding can help you raise children who thrive.* Tarcher/Penguin.
- Silk, J. S., Morris, A. S., Kanaya, T., & Steinberg, L. (2003). Psychological control and autonomy granting: Opposite ends of a continuum or distinct constructs? *Journal of Research on Adolescence, 13*(1), 113–128.
- Soenens, B., & Vansteenkiste, M. (2010). A theoretical upgrade of the concept of parental psychological control: Proposing new insights on the basis of self-determination theory. *Developmental Review, 30*(1), 74–99.
- Steinberg, L. (2001). We know some things: Parent-adolescent relationships in retrospect and prospect. *Journal of Research on Adolescence, 11*(1), 1–19.
- Steinberg, L. (2014). *Age of opportunity: Lessons from the new science of adolescence.* Houghton Mifflin Harcourt.
- Substance Abuse and Mental Health Services Administration. (2025, September 26). *988 Suicide & Crisis Lifeline.*
- Twenge, J. M. (2017). *iGen: Why today's super-connected kids are growing up less rebellious, more tolerant, less happy—and completely unprepared for adulthood.* Atria Books.
- Weinstein, E., & James, C. (2022). *Behind their screens: What teens are facing (and adults are missing).* MIT Press.
- Whitlock, J., Muehlenkamp, J., & Eckenrode, J. (2008). Variation in nonsuicidal self-injury: Identification and features of latent classes in a

college population of emerging adults. *Journal of Clinical Child & Adolescent Psychology, 37*(4), 725–735.

www.ingramcontent.com/pod-product-compliance
Lightning Source LLC
Chambersburg PA
CBHW062039090426
42740CB00016B/2955